MW01146625

# The Cost
# of Ambition

# Theology for the Life of the World

Jesus Christ is God come to dwell among humans, to be, to speak, and to act "for the life of the world" (John 6:51). Taking its mandate from the character and mission of God, Christian theology's task is to discern, articulate, and commend visions of flourishing life in light of God's self-revelation in Jesus Christ. The Theology for the Life of the World series features texts that do just that.

Human life is diverse and multifaceted, and so will be the books in this series. Some will focus on one specific aspect of life. Others will elaborate expansive visions of human persons, social life, or the world in relation to God. All will share the conviction that theology is vital to exploring the character of true life in diverse settings and orienting us toward it. No task is greater than for each of us and all of us together to discern and pursue the flourishing of all in God's creation. These books are meant as a contribution to that task.

# The Cost of Ambition

## How Striving to Be Better Than Others Makes Us Worse

## Miroslav Volf

**Brazos Press**

*a division of Baker Publishing Group*
Grand Rapids, Michigan

Published by Brazos Press
a division of Baker Publishing Group
Grand Rapids, Michigan
BrazosPress.com

Printed in the United States of America

Library of Congress Cataloging-in-Publication Data
Names: Volf, Miroslav, author.
Title: The cost of ambition : how striving to be better than others makes us worse / Miroslav Volf.
Description: Grand Rapids, Michigan : Brazos Press, a division of Baker Publishing Group, [2025] | Series: Theology for the life of the world | Includes bibliographical references.
Identifiers: LCCN 2024045347 | ISBN 9781587434815 (cloth) | ISBN 9781587434822 (paperback) | ISBN 9781493450343 (ebook)
Subjects: LCSH: Success—Religious aspects—Christianity. | Ambition.
Classification: LCC BV4598.3 .V65 2025 | DDC 248.4—dc23/eng/20241123
LC record available at https://lccn.loc.gov/2024045347

Cover design by Darren Welch Design

Author is represented by the Martell Agency.

Baker Publishing Group publications use paper produced from sustainable forestry practices and postconsumer waste whenever possible.

25   26   27   28   29   30   31          7   6   5   4   3   2   1

*To Ryan*

Beware of the scribes, who like to walk around in long robes and to be greeted with respect in the marketplaces and to have the best seats in the synagogues and places of honor at banquets! They devour widows' houses and for the sake of appearance say long prayers.

—Jesus (Mark 12:38–40)

"Love," says my Lord Rochfaucault, "is commonly succeeded by ambition; but ambition is hardly ever succeeded by love." That passion, when once it has got entire possession of the breast, will admit neither a rival nor a successor.

—Adam Smith, *The Theory of Moral Sentiments*

Pride is essentially competitive. . . . Pride gets no pleasure out of having something, only out of having more of it than the next man. We say that people are proud of being rich, or clever, or good-looking, but they are not. They are proud of being richer, or cleverer, or better looking than others.

—C. S. Lewis, *Mere Christianity*

Mira (as she saw that she was losing): "I don't want to play anymore!"
I: "But when you win, someone else loses!"
Mira: "There should not be games in which *anyone* loses!"

—My daughter, when she was five

# Contents

# Preface

I am not sure when I started thinking that striving to be better than someone else—striving for superiority—is a problem. "Started" might not be quite the right word. Perhaps a better way to put the uncertainty would be to say that I don't know when I abandoned the heresy that striving for superiority is a great good and returned to the implicit "faith" of my early childhood. I never heard my parents or my saintly nanny encourage me to outdo anyone in anything or praise me for having done so. In the Volf household, as I later realized, it was assumed that we ought to do things well— that the apartment ought to be impeccably clean (my mother) and the chocolate spread on the torte perfectly flat and the intricate icing just right (my father). Whether we did things better than others should not matter; other people were not our measure. It often did, of course, matter, certainly for me—and, to my shame, it still does.

I first publicly argued that striving for superiority is not as valuable as often assumed in October 2019 at the Second Global Congress on Sport and Christianity in Grand Rapids, Michigan. In my keynote address, I expanded on an unpopular thesis: though the monetary and reputational value of successfully striving for superiority in sport can be great—Lionel Messi, then the highest-earning athlete and among the most famous people in the world, was my example—the *moral* value of such striving is, at best, questionable. Accompanied as it often is by chest-beating and I-am-the-greatest kind of strutting, striving for superiority seemed to me at odds not just with my parents' example but, more importantly, with the spirit and the letter of the Christian faith, an affront against the humility that ought to mark it. When choosing the topic of my address, I thought to myself, Let's stir up some controversy!

After the lecture, the problem of striving for superiority would not let go of me—the tension between the goods that come from it, on the one hand, and the actual damage to ourselves and our world that it causes, on the other. Consider just two examples. One comes from the history of ethical growth. At the end of *Cosmic Connections*, Charles Taylor traces the historical working out of core ethical insights common to human beings. He notes that some important insights "have bred egregious self-images of superiority over other peoples and civilizations, which have in turn legitimized much injustice."[1] A sense of European superiority both inferiorized other peoples and legitimized centuries of violence against them, most horrendously exemplified in the slave trade.

The other example is about the effects of striving for superiority on our sense of self-worth. (For a more comprehensive list, see theses 6–18 in the conclusion.) Yale students are a privileged group and, one would assume, comfortable in their own skins. Most of them are exceptionally talented, hardworking, and accomplished. Many graduated at the very top of their class in high school. But when they arrive at Yale, each becomes just one of five thousand similarly distinguished students. For some, this leveling experience is disorienting; comparison with their peers no longer turns as often to their advantage as they had learned to expect. They had derived much of their self-worth from being among the very best, and now, immersed in a crowd of rough equals—most of whom are in some regard their superiors—their self-esteem plummets. Accustomed to being superior, they feel the sharp sting of inferiority.

A sense of inferiority fuels striving for superiority, and striving for superiority is shadowed by feelings of both pride and inferiority. We oscillate between "I am better than some, maybe even most!" and "Everybody is better than me—or at least everyone who matters." Behind the oscillation is an unstated conviction: "I must be at least better than most—beyond average—or I am inadequate, a loser, nothing." And still further back behind that conviction is yet another: "My worth derives from how I stack up against others; I *am* how I stack up against others."

I hope to show that it is possible to break out of the self-reinforcing oscillation between the sense of inferiority and striving for superiority, wrest our self-worth from captivity to comparisons with others, and live confidently, out of a well of living water at the bedrock of our souls, undaunted by how we stack up against others. If we do, for each of us and all of us together, a new world will dawn.

———※———

I have come to believe that biblical traditions and important theological thinkers can help open our eyes to see striving for superiority for the ill it is and nudge us to strive joyfully for genuine goods—for what these goods are in themselves and for their benefits to ourselves, others, and the world.

It takes only a quick perusal through the Bible to see that striving for superiority is a dominant theme in the story of human suffering and wrongdoing. Consider Cain, the beloved firstborn of the mother of all humans, and his relation to his younger brother, Abel. Giving birth to Cain, Eve exclaims, "I have produced a man with the help of the LORD" (Gen. 4:1). She is less elated with her second son and names him Abel, which means "vapor," a mere mist blown by the wind. When the Lord upends the order of preeminence by accepting the offering of the lesser Abel rather than that of the preferred Cain, Cain kills his sibling rival (4:1–16). At the other end of the Bible, in the book of Revelation, consider the beast with ten horns and seven heads, the incarnation of evil. John the Seer writes that the whole world is filled with wonder over its invincible power and worships it, exclaiming, "Who is like the beast, and who can fight against it?" (Rev. 13:4). The beast's strength is superior to everyone's.

The Bible is thus bookended by humans' obsession with superiority —and by murder and war, extremes of the measures to which people resort to attain it and keep it. And between these stories from Genesis to Revelation, the theme recurs over and over. When two of my primary interlocutors, John Milton and Søren Kierkegaard, write about the evils of striving for superiority and sketch alternatives to it, they are, above all, interpreting the Bible. And when Paul, my third main interlocutor, does the same, he is *writing* the Bible!

As I was writing this book, exploring what the Hebrew Bible, Jesus, Paul, Milton, and Kierkegaard say about striving for superiority, the sentences I wrote had a way of turning around and talking back to me—not only to my intellect but also to my heart, the hearth where the flame of ambition burns. I hope this book will speak to you as well: through Kierkegaard's contented little lily, which, though more beautiful than Solomon in all his splendor, became distraught at not being a Crown Imperial, the queen of the lilies; through the boundless ambition of Milton's Satan, his self-loathing, and his final fall from the pinnacle of the temple; through Paul's realization that in trying to be the best he was "rubbishing" God's gifts, or through the intentional madness of his own boasting in a farcical attempt to persuade the Corinthians that boasting is foolish. I found what the Hebrew Scriptures, Jesus, Paul, Milton, and Kierkegaard have to say fascinating, profound, and life-changing. Writing this book was a spiritual exercise, a transformation of the mind and, even more, of the heart. My hope is that reading it may be that for you as well.

I designed the book such that you can start reading it at the beginning or at the end, with chapter 1 or with the twenty-three theses on striving for superiority that make up the conclusion. You can also start with any of the chapters in the middle. Each is self-contained, and each offers a distinctive take on striving for superiority, highlighting aspects of its problems and of the alternatives to it. The chapters also complement one another, as I will suggest in the brief summary of the book in the conclusion.

# 1

# "O Solomon,
# I Have Outdone You!"

## 1

"Glory be to God who considered me worthy of this task! O Solomon, I have outdone you!" So the Roman emperor Justinian the Great (527–62) is reported to have exclaimed on December 26, 537. Most of us are nothing like Justinian in stature, yet we can recognize his desire to outdo a competitor, small or large, as our own.

Accompanied by the patriarch and a multitude of the faithful, Justinian made the triumphant exclamation as he was consecrating Hagia Sophia, the stunning archetype of Byzantine architecture, a project into which he had poured a great deal of energy and resources, hovering over the design and construction like a hawk. The exclamation is likely apocryphal, but the striving for superiority to which it gives expression was genuine and fierce.[1] He thought he had proven himself superior to Solomon, the builder of Israel's first temple and, according to the book Justinian regarded as holy, a man of unmatchable wisdom. Solomon, too, had been competing for superiority. The house that was to be built for the God who "is greater than other gods" had to be, his father, King David, instructed him, "exceedingly magnificent, famous and glorified throughout all lands" (2 Chron. 2:5; 1 Chron. 22:5). The greatness of his God and the majesty of the house he was to build for God were both to redound to Solomon's superiority. And Justinian, in completing Hagia Sophia, had proven himself superior to Solomon.

Justinian was not the one who had started the building competition with Solomon in Constantinople. In 527, Anicia Juliana, a descendant of Western emperors and a woman of great wealth, had completed a majestic building of her own, the Church of St. Polyeuktos. When the church was built, it "was the largest and most sumptuous church in the city."[2] It was decorated with palm trees, pomegranates, vine scrolls, open flowers, and capitals shaped like lilies—all themes drawn straight from the biblical descriptions of Solomon's temple.[3] Moreover, one hundred cubits square (a biblical standard unit of measure, not a Roman one!), the church was designed to resemble the yet greater eschatological temple of Ezekiel's visions.[4] In scale and costliness, Juliana's church exceeded any other church in the capital at the time of construction.[5] The dedicatory poem for the church includes the line "She [Juliana] alone did violence to time and surpassed the wisdom of renowned Solomon by raising a habitation for God."[6]

The Church of St. Polyeuktos was dedicated in the year of Justinian's accession to the throne. It must have been a thorn in his flesh, especially as Juliana was a descendant of Roman royalty, while he was of Illyrian peasant stock. And then there was her large fortune. He wanted her to contribute part of it to the state treasury. She stalled—and then melted much of her gold into plates with which she adorned the interior of the roof of her church.

Justinian's opportunity to outdo Juliana came in 532 when another church was destroyed by fire during the Nika Riots. The plans for the new church were ready in forty days, "suggesting that there had been considerable prior preparation even before the Nika Riots had actually made necessary the rebuilding of the church."[7] Completed after only five years of work at a breakneck pace and with unstinting funding from the emperor, the edifice was a breathtaking achievement. The church was twice the size of Juliana's, and it dwarfed Solomon's temple. According to 1 Kings 6, Solomon's temple was 27.43 meters long, 9.14 meters wide, and 17.73 meters high and took seven years to complete. Justinian's Hagia Sophia was twenty-four times the footprint area of Solomon's temple, was fifty-five meters tall, and took only five years to complete. More importantly, architectural advances and its novel design meant that the building let in a tremendous amount of light compared to its predecessors, including the Roman Pantheon. Streaming in through multiple windows at different angles, light flooded the space and interacted brilliantly with its surfaces—large expanses of marble floor and extraordinary stretches of polychrome mosaics running across curved and straight surfaces. It was an earthly new Jerusalem, a space worthy to be God's dwelling.[8]

Justinian thus surpassed both his ancient rival, Solomon, and his contemporary rival, Juliana. With his church built, he could even boast that he had made Constantinople, the new capital of the empire, surpass Rome, the old capital. The poet and courtier to Justinian, Paul the Silentiary (d. ca. 575), boasted for him: "By raising this infinite temple about your arm, he has made you [Constantinople] more brilliant than your mother on the Tiber who bore you. Give way, I say, renowned Roman Capitol, give way! My Emperor has so far overtopped that wonder as great God is superior to an idol!"[9]

Splendiferous as Hagia Sophia was, the problems with the design and the rushed construction, partly the effects of striving for superiority, began to show almost immediately. Robert Ousterhout describes in detail the ways the unprecedented weight of the building exacerbated structural defects. In addition, the haste of construction meant building on top of mortar that had not yet fully dried, creating a situation of "plastic flow" leading to permanent deformation.[10] Attempts were made to correct these issues as construction advanced, but, ultimately, an earthquake in 557 led to the collapse of the dome.[11] Juliana had died in 527 and could neither be humiliated by the great church nor experience *Schadenfreude* when its dome collapsed. The building has been repaired several times since, but it is still largely continuous with that rebuilt structure, designed by the son of one of the original architects and rededicated in 562 by a presumably chastened Justinian.[12]

Excellence and upmanship pursued together; magnificence achieved and failure suffered at the same time; extortion and exploitation along with great artisanship and dedication; gratitude to God expressed in the same breath as hubristic, almost fantastical, rivalry. Such are some of the problems of Justinian's striving for superiority.

The problems expand when we consider the character of the God in whose honor Justinian, Juliana, and Solomon built their temples. David and Solomon's idea that the greatness of God's "house" should reflect the greatness of God seems plausible until we remember that God is *incomparably greater*—and in an entirely different category of greatness—than the gods. Because God is the Creator of everything, "even highest heaven" cannot contain God, as Solomon himself stated (2 Chron. 2:6). It is hard not to hear God's pushback, through the prophet Nathan, when David originally suggested the idea of building a temple for God. God did not request it. God acquiesced to it just as God acquiesced to monarchy (2 Sam. 7:1–16).

As for Juliana's and Justinian's competition with each other as well as with Solomon, it contradicted the very capstone and cornerstone of their faith, even if the beauty of the edifices they created gestured toward the glory of Christian eschatological hope.[13] Central to the Christian faith is the conviction that the God of Israel, the master of the universe, came to dwell first in

4

the womb of a lowly woman from Nazareth and then in a more abiding way in the child to whom she gave birth. The body of that "marginal Jew," who had no place to lay his head, was the most exalted temple of God (John 2:21). The highest one became as the lowliest ones are. The humility of love is a central aspect of God's glory facing humanity. This, then, was the irreconcilable incongruity in Juliana and Justinian's rivalry: they were striving for superiority over each other by building temples in honor of the God whose essential humility they were thereby failing to honor.

=≡≡=

As the popularity of sports suggests, today striving for superiority is widespread, perhaps especially in the United States. The culture of athletic contests partly reflects and partly stimulates a more general striving for superiority in politics, economics, education, arts, and even ordinary life.[14] President Obama put the cultural effects of sport well, and approvingly. What attracts people to sports, he noted, is that "it's one of the few places where it's a true meritocracy. There's not a lot of BS. Ultimately, who's winning, who's losing, who's performing, who's not—it's all laid out there."[15] Striving for superiority regulated by meritocracy—that is the ideal, in sports and in most other domains of life, with which people identify.

Striving for superiority is not just what the great and eminent do—royalty, like Solomon, Juliana, and Justinian—or those who imagine themselves as such. Nor does it happen only within delineated domains of life, like sports or markets, under stable rules. Striving for superiority is literally everywhere. I am getting from terminal B to terminal C in Chicago O'Hare Airport, and instead of taking the escalators and the moving walkways, I walk with my small suitcase and bag of books, descend sixty stairs, continue walking the entire length of the tunnel underpass along the moving walkway, and, on the other end, ascend sixty stairs—and I feel a bit superior to the masses who aren't exercising and are burning fossil fuels rather than calories. (This, of course, is crazy, because I know nothing about the exercise patterns of any of these people, their relation to fossil fuels, let alone the state of their health or their incapacities that may make them prefer moving walkways and escalators. And how environmentally virtuous can my refusal to burn fossil fuels be, given that I have just landed and am rushing to catch another plane!?) Or as we drive our perfectly good car—say, a budget Honda—into our garage, we see a brand new Audi parked in front of our neighbor's house, and we feel our car devalued and ourselves diminished. We look over at our neighbor to the other side and see their much older Honda with worse gas mileage, and we feel slightly better; at least our car is better than theirs, making us superior to them.

We compare our virtue and our wealth, our attire and looks, our success as scholars or our power as influencers, the tone of our muscles and the number of our social media "likes," the range of our friends and the lands of our origin, or, if we are super-billionaires, the sophistication and reach of our rockets—and in all of this, we often place ourselves on a single scale of value, hoping for the short-lived exhilaration of finding ourselves above our competitors, not necessarily above all of them but at least above some relevant rivals. If we find ourselves below them, we feel the sting of inferiority, envy burrows itself into our soul, and we strive to catch up and overtake them or hope that someone will loosen the criteria so that we too can get an A lest, as is increasingly the case, the dogged demons of depression come to occupy our soul, the poisonous progeny of our sense of inadequacy. You might think that our troubles and our striving would end if we reached a state of near equality with others. They won't. Every state of equality achieved through competition is unstable. And so our striving to catch up and overtake—and suffering when we fail—continues.

By now you have gathered that by striving for superiority I mean striving to be better than someone else, not simply striving to be better. At the end of this chapter, I will explore this definition in greater detail—the differences between striving for superiority and striving for excellence, between being better at something and being better as a person, between the moral value of striving for superiority and the monetary value (see sec. 5). But first I need to say more about (1) what is at stake in living so comfortably with, and even celebrating, striving for superiority (sec. 2), (2) how prevalent and relentless the striving has become, especially in late modernity (secs. 2 and 3), and (3) how deeply it affects our lives in many domains (sec. 4).

**2**

Though we swim in waters colored by striving for superiority, we are often like the two young fish in the now famous parable David Foster Wallace told at the beginning of his 2005 commencement address on the compassionate life. As an older fish passes by two younger fish swimming the other way, it nods at them and says, "'Morning, boys. How's the water?' And the two young fish swim for a bit, and then eventually one of them looks over at the other and goes, 'What the hell is water?'"[16] The young fish don't see and therefore aren't concerned about what envelops them from all sides. Why should we be aware of and possibly concerned about the striving for superiority in which we all swim?

There is an ancient and now half-forgotten disagreement about whether striving for superiority is a life-giving ingredient, a dangerous pollutant, or perhaps a bit of both. At the beginning of his didactic poem *Works and Days*, the Greek poet Hesiod, who lived around 700 BC, sings praises to the good Eris, the goddess of striving for superiority. He knows very well that there is also a bad Eris, the goddess of the kind of rivalry that issues in "wicked war and feuding." The bad Eris is "a cruel thing," deserving condemnation. But the good Eris is of a very different disposition. After noting that it was Zeus who placed the good Eris on the roots of the earth and among humans, Hesiod writes,

> She drives even the unskilled man to work; and if someone who lacks property sees someone else who is rich, he likewise hurries off to sow and plant and set his house in order; neighbor competes with neighbor for prosperity. This Eris is good for men. Even potters harbour grudges against potters, carpenters against carpenters, beggars envy beggars and minstrels envy minstrels.[17]

Striving for superiority and the envy that drives it contribute not just to the development of individuals. Progress in crafts, arts, and sciences is predicated on them, Hesiod claims. Zeus had wisely placed the good Eris at the very roots of the earth; many good things grow from it.

Important strands of the biblical tradition stand in sharp contrast to Hesiod's praise of striving for superiority. The ancient writer Qohelet, identified often as King Solomon, agrees with Hesiod that "all toil and all skill in work come from one person's envy of another" (Eccles. 4:4). But in Qohelet's world, "the race is not to the swift, nor the battle to the strong, nor bread to the wise, nor riches to the intelligent, nor favor to the skillful, but time and chance happen to them all" (9:11). His point is not only that those with superior skill and power sometimes lose but also that even when they win, their victories are pyrrhic. For all their industry, they ultimately end up empty-handed. Skill and toil in work born of striving for superiority are "vanity and a chasing after wind," no matter how impressive their results may turn out to be (4:4).

In the ancient texts of the Western tradition, we have these two contrasting views of striving for superiority. One tradition considers it a source of personal and cultural progress. In the other, it is a deceptively attractive means by which false glory, empty and harmful, is enthroned among humans.

More than two millennia later, in the *Discourse on the Origin and the Foundation of Inequality among Men*, known simply as the *Second Discourse*, Jean-Jacques Rousseau joins the two traditions into a tense marriage. He clearly prefers one partner to the other, though how exactly Rousseau assesses the moral corruption and cultural advances that result from striving for superiority is a matter of scholarly debate.[18] His interest in the topic arises from a concern to preserve human freedom "in a world where people are increasingly dependent on one another to satisfy their needs."[19] Rousseau is likely the most significant and most influential modern critic of striving for superiority.

Rousseau distinguishes famously between two kinds of love a person has for themselves: *amour de soi-même* and *amour propre*. The first is simple to translate: self-love. He describes it as "a natural sentiment that inclines every animal to attend to its self-preservation and that, guided in man by reason and modified by pity, produces humanity and virtue." The second kind of love, *amour propre*, is impossible to translate and therefore remains mostly untranslated. Roughly, he means by it a desire for preeminence. He describes it as "only a relative sentiment, factitious and born in society."[20] *Amour propre* is "relative" because it arises in social settings as people compare themselves to one another. It is "factitious" because it gives rise to strife. As to its birth in society, here is how Rousseau describes it. At the point in the development of humanity when contacts among humans expanded and bonds between them tightened,

> everyone began to look at everyone else and to wish to be looked at himself, and public esteem acquired a value. The one who sang or danced the best; the handsomest, the strongest, the most skillful or the most eloquent came to be the most highly regarded, and this was the first step at once toward inequality and vice: from these first preferences arose vanity and contempt on the one hand, shame and envy on the other; and the ferment caused by these

9

new leavens eventually produced compounds fatal to happiness and innocence.[21]

Once the idea of esteem was formed—the idea of being looked at and assessed as superior or inferior in comparative terms—everyone aspired to avoid contempt and be regarded well; ultimately, they aspired to be "most highly regarded." This aspiration was, Rousseau believed, "the first step at once toward inequality and vice."[22]

Once esteem became valuable, "everyone claimed a right to it, and it was no longer possible to deprive anyone of it with impunity." In many instances, the contempt of the person became more difficult to bear than physical injury. And from this arose a desire for terrible, bloodthirsty revenge. To curb it, though, from the same source arose "the first duties of civility."[23] Striving for superiority is the source of both vice and virtue. We owe to it, Rousseau writes later in his story of humanity, "what is best and what is worst among men, our virtues and our vices, our Sciences and our errors, our Conquerors and our Philosophers."[24] Reading this both-and sentence, we may be tempted to conclude that in Rousseau's mind negative and positive effects are roughly balanced. But that would be a mistake. That same sentence concludes: "a multitude of bad things and a *small number of good*."[25]

Though the goal of the *Second Discourse* is to trace the origin and identify the foundation of human inequality, this last sentence and the very end of the book suggest that Rousseau's deeper concern is the social conditions of his time. In modern times—and here that means the middle of the eighteenth century—the "petulant activity of our *amour propre*"[26] accentuates its bad effects. It enslaves humans.[27] It forces them to toil in the prison house of the overwhelming need to measure up to the evaluative gaze of others. It leads to futile and unending labor to equal or to best others and gain social esteem. The person striving for superiority is "always outside himself, is capable of living only in the opinion of others

10

and, so to speak, derives the sentiment of his own existence solely from their judgment." Worse,

> everything [is] being reduced to appearances, everything becomes contrivance and play-acting; honor, friendship, virtue, and often even vices in which one at length discovers the secret of glorying; how, in a word, forever asking others what we are without ever daring to ask it of ourselves, in the midst of so much Philosophy, humanity, politeness, and Sublime maxims, we have nothing more than a deceiving and frivolous exterior, honor without virtue, reason without wisdom and pleasure without happiness.[28]

This is Qohelet plus! Striving for superiority is here not mere futility. It is a chasing after wind that creates a culture of pernicious vacuity. Whatever cultural and material and even intellectual progress striving for superiority stimulates, these gains are not worth the hollowing out of human life it causes. Rousseau exaggerates: *all* "honor, friendship, virtue" are mere contrivance and play-acting, he claims. Yet, reading the passage, we have a sense that he is describing *us*, our lives on social media, for instance.

**3**

Rousseau's brief but searing critique of striving for superiority seems to be more relevant today than when he penned it almost three centuries ago. In modern societies, the pressure of comparison, competition, and craving to be at least a bit better than others has intensified. In Rousseau's *Second Discourse*—as in the thought of Adam Smith[29] and in that of Thomas Hobbes, who preceded both by more than a century[30]—striving for superiority appears as a drive native to humans as social animals. Today, such a drive has been "enhanced" into a potent psychic fuel that helps power most domains of our lives, a key ingredient propelling what Harmut Rosa has called the systematic "logic of increase" that is characteristic of social life in modernity.[31]

In the transition from premodern to modern societies, the character of striving for superiority has transformed. Just consider how the character of human desires more generally has changed. For a good source of understanding desire in premodern societies we can return to Qohelet. Likening the human person to a sea, Qohelet writes, "All streams run to the sea, but the sea is not full; to the place where the streams flow, there they continue to flow. . . . The eye is not satisfied with seeing or the ear filled with hearing" (Eccles. 1:7–8). Qohelet believes it isn't in human nature to halt anywhere in possession and enjoyment and to be abidingly satisfied.[32] We are finite, but our desires seem nearly infinite, always beyond the edge of our reach. The insatiability of desire notwithstanding, concrete desires, say, for the material goods that humans pursued in premodern times, remained relatively limited. More importantly, those desires largely preceded the goods toward which they were directed. A person has a need; there is an object that will satisfy it; desire mediates between the person and that object.

Modern desire does not work quite this way. In his classic *The Affluent Society*, John Kenneth Galbraith notes that a modern market economy does not so much respond to existing needs by producing goods that will satisfy them as it "creates the wants the goods are presumed to satisfy"; it "fills the void that it has itself created."[33] A modern economy *generates* desires—*our* desires—so that it can satisfy them. Insinuating itself into the crevices of our hearts, it does the desiring for us and in us. Anyone seduced by the algorithm to scroll for longer than they intended has experienced an alien force operating as their very own desire.

In the course of modernity, the character of striving for superiority has changed in a similar way to how the character of desire has changed. We live in societies in which competing with others is an objective condition of life in education, economy, politics, arts, sciences, and more, as I will illustrate shortly. Many of us have become entrepreneurs of our own selves whose survival and thriving depend on our ability to outcompete others. If we fail, we may languish; in extreme cases we may even die. We are under pressure to strive for superiority over our competitors. More often than not, there are no objective standards of excellence. What counts as excellent is a moving target, as in sports, set by the competition itself; you are excellent when you are near equal or marginally superior to relevant others. Under such conditions, we integrate striving for superiority into our own value system and our sense of identity.

Striving to be better than others has become an integral part not just of our values but of our identity and therefore of our desires. When we have outdone others, we are proud—and anxious, for every success is temporary and can be secured only by the same means it has been achieved. When others have outdone us, we feel inadequate, inferiorized—made uncertain of not just whether we can perform a task but whether as human beings we are adequate. Unsurprisingly, depression has become a signature psychological disorder over the past fifty years or so. As Alain Ehrenberg argues in *The Weariness of the Self*, depression is "a malady of inadequacy" afflicting those who have a painful sense of failing to achieve—by being better than others.[34]

## 4.

This malady of inadequacy is acutely felt in many areas of our lives.[35] I will illustrate this by looking briefly at three contemporary domains where striving for superiority has deleterious and depressing effects: social media, education, and politics. I suspect many of us will resonate with these descriptions of how the ubiquitous quest for superiority has made us worse.

━━ ⅲ ━━

The negative effects of social media on mental health are well-documented. In May 2023, the surgeon general of the United States issued an advisory highlighting many of the risks for adolescents in particular.[36] The risks are complex and multifaceted, including everything from exposure to various kinds of harmful content to questions of time use and the interruption of other daily activities. One key risk concerns the way social media heightens comparison. While humans always engage in social comparison of various kinds, social media sharply heightens these dynamics. It drives comparison on nearly every axis imaginable (physical appearance, musical talent, wittiness, erudition, popularity, wealth, mathematical skills, capacity to eat a large number of eggs in one sitting . . . ); it presents others in highly curated forms and in ways directly measured by "likes" and comments; and it does this at our fingertips, in a constant barrage, rewarding us for engaging more and more with the content. These comparisons inevitably leave us discontented with ourselves and either striving to gain superiority or despairing at our inability to do so.

Speaking specifically about teen girls, the surgeon general notes that social comparison driven by social media "is associated with body dissatisfaction, disordered eating, and depressive symptoms."[37] But similar effects can apply to each of us. Theologians, for example, are confronted with images of their peers' offices and bookshelves—only the ones thought beautiful and full enough to be shared publicly, of course—and may be left feeling either inferior or newly motivated to strive for superiority. Or they may be stung when met with a list of accomplishments from other figures in the field: a new book that is selling well, an upcoming conference talk, a brilliant new idea published in a forthcoming paper. The line between keeping abreast of the field and intense personal comparison and jockeying for position is often a slender one. But social media heightens our ability to compare and our desire to fight for superiority in a way only possible in modernity—with devastating consequences for our sense of security, our mental health, the sorts of pursuits we devote our time to, and even our sense of self.

Social media might seem like too easy an example. But striving for superiority has infiltrated and poisoned even such fundamentally worthwhile pursuits as education. Numerous commentators have observed the rapid decline in admissions rates at top US colleges and universities. This is due to both increasing numbers of applicants and higher standards for admission, but the bottom line is the same: competition increases as more students vie for the superior status of elite education. As with social media, the key casualty of this competition is the mental health of the ever-younger students asked to build their lives around their future college applications. A number of studies show that "youth growing up in the context of high-achieving schools . . . are statistically more likely than normative samples to show serious disturbances across several domains including drug and alcohol use, as well as internalizing and externalizing problems."[38] Despite the typical status and material well-being of these children, the competition they are caught in has deleterious effects on their mental health. The authors of a review paper make no bones about what they see as the underlying cause of these maladies, attributing it to "the pervasive emphasis, in contemporary American culture, on maximizing personal status and how this can threaten the well-being of individuals and of communities."[39]

This striving for superiority is deleterious for more than just its participants. As recent admissions cheating scandals have shown, it degrades the good for which people compete as well. In the introduction to *The Tyranny of Merit*, Michael Sandel reviews the story of how William Singer engaged in illicit means—such as bribing test proctors and sports coaches—to help secure admission for children of his wealthy clients.[40] Of course, something not entirely dissimilar happens all the time, as the children of big donors and alumni get various sorts of preference. More generally, enrollment at selective schools is highly correlated with income, as "more than two-thirds of students at Ivy League schools come from the top 20 percent of the income scale; at Princeton and Yale, more students come from the top 1 percent than from the entire bottom 60 percent of the country."[41] This entanglement with questions of merit and status, Sandel notes, represents a shift in the purpose of higher education. As admission to elite schools becomes increasingly a matter of pure status and of insurance against economic volatility, the focus drifts away from education for its own sake. One pursues victory, not simply educational attainment—or, perhaps, students at these elite schools sometimes feel free to pursue the subjects that interest them because they have already won the race for admission and are nigh guaranteed a job no matter what they study! Either way, once higher education becomes reified as the object of striving for superiority, it begins to lose its original charge and its unstated purpose becomes status. Striving for superiority, even in values and attainments that are excellent themselves, can erode that very excellence.

＝＝ ⚏ ＝＝

Politics, too, has been shaped by the demands of striving for superiority. As we are flooded with an endless cycle of information, politics has become assimilated to the demands of the attention economy. Though always about power and influence, today politics increasingly revolves around pure competition. Dominance has replaced the common good as the aim of governance. One of the many casualties has been the role of truth in public discourse: leaders become incentivized to say whatever they think will help keep them in power. In 2018, RAND published a report on "Truth Decay," which made the summer reading list of former president Obama.[42] Defined as "the diminishing role of, trust in, and respect for facts, data, and analysis" in "political and civil discourse,"[43] truth decay was found to be intertwined with increasing polarization and the erosion of civil discourse. The implications for the behavior of our elected leaders are unsurprising. A recent study suggests that preferences for truth telling among politicians are negatively correlated with getting reelected.[44] When superiority in the form of popularity and thus electoral victory becomes its own good, it tends to create its own rules of engagement, its own internal goods, its own standards of value—and reality itself becomes eclipsed.

=⊞=

My brief comments on social media, education, and politics suggest that striving for superiority is pervasive, clothed in distinctively modern and deeply pernicious guise. They also highlight some of the harmful effects of such striving that I will examine in the pages to follow. Striving for superiority over others creates the feelings of inferiority that it purports to solve; it is highly contagious in cultural systems and social structures; it creates distortive and deceptive views of reality; and it incentivizes the pursuit of low-value goods for the sake of status and minimizes the value of excellence.

## 5

Thus far, I have said a lot about striving for superiority, but I have not yet detailed what it is. To explain how I am using the term, I need to make some distinctions. (The discussion here is a bit more technical, and if you keep in mind that striving for superiority is about being better than someone else and not just better for the sake of being better, you can skip this section and read the rest of the book. You may then want to return to these pages if you get puzzled about such things as the relation between the moral and the instrumental value of striving for superiority or between striving to be better at something and striving to be better as a person.)

=⊞=

*Comparison versus competition.* Comparison can mean as little as simply noting similarities or differences between whatever it is we are comparing. As I am turning into my driveway, I note differences between the Audi (let's say it is a new electric model) that is parked in my neighbor's driveway and the Honda in which I am sitting.

17

Since I know something about these two kinds of cars, I recognize that the Audi is a much better car in most regards. In evaluating the two cars, I am comparing not only the features of the two cars but also their relative value. "My neighbor has a better car than I have" is a comparative statement of value, not a competitive one. Once I start desiring to have a car that is at least as good as my neighbor's, or even just to narrow the gap in quality between our cars, I am no longer just comparing. I have moved from the green zone of comparing to *potentially* the red zone of competing with my neighbor whose car has become my measure. I am now striving to have a car closer in perceived goodness to his, if not equal or better.

Why are we mostly not satisfied with simply comparing and learning from comparisons? Why do we strive to outdo one another? For my purposes, I can leave the ultimate explanation of striving for superiority undetermined. Perhaps I am striving for superiority because Adam and Eve, having been beguiled by the ultimate striver for superiority, Satan, desired to be both like God and better than each other and bequeathed to me the same misdirected desire. This is what Milton, along with much of Christian tradition, thought (see chap. 3). Perhaps I acquired the desire in society, as we have seen Jean-Jacques Rousseau thought. Had humanity stayed in the state of nature, I would not be striving for superiority, but since I live in society, I have come to desire to be better than others, perhaps even the best, to be "the most highly regarded."[45] Or perhaps such desire is natural to me because the ancient struggle for survival has inscribed it into the very fabric of my being.[46] Perhaps all these are in play. Whatever the reason, often I am not just comparing my car with my neighbor's. I am craving to have a car at least as good and hopefully better, to somehow best them, if not in the cars we drive then in some other, perhaps to me more important, regard—or at least I tend to do so unless I impose on myself some form of spiritual discipline.

*Striving for excellence versus striving for superiority.* Striving for excellence means striving to become better in some regard, to improve, or at least not to get worse, especially as we age;[47] it is striving to be *better than myself.* Striving for superiority, in contrast, is striving to be *better than someone else*, which can range from being better than my sibling, neighbor, or school friend to being better than anyone living, even to become the GOAT—the greatest of all time. As I understand them, these are two crucially different strivings.

Striving for excellence is indexed either to some objective standard I seek to approximate and perhaps exceed or to some goal I have designed and set for myself. The standard itself can be worthwhile (like giving half of my income or securing access to clean water for those who don't have it), trivial (like the aspiration to have all ten of my fingernails be at least 5 cm long), or pernicious (like the desire to amass a large arsenal of nuclear weapons). If in striving for excellence I compete at all, I compete against myself. The achievements of others are of secondary interest. Seeing my neighbor's new Audi electric car, for instance, can remind me that I have committed myself to switching from a combustion engine to more sustainable, eco-friendly sort of car and set me back on track pursuing that goal.

Striving for superiority, in contrast, is essentially competitive (more on this below). It differs also because striving for superiority is not inherently tied to improvement at all, whether of a worthwhile, trivial, or pernicious kind. I can become better than someone else by that person becoming worse or by obstructing the performance of my competitor. It is even possible for everyone to become worse and for me still to become better than everyone else. Striving for superiority often involves striving to be better oneself, but it does not need to and can be inimical to it. Hence, striving for superiority is categorically distinct from striving for excellence.[48]

To make the difference between striving for superiority and striving for excellence clear, it may help to eliminate two ways of distinguishing the two. First, the distinction is not that striving for superiority involves *comparisons*, whereas striving for excellence does not. In many cases, striving for excellence will also involve comparing. In sports or arts, there are no objective standards of excellence. The standards of excellence change with the evolving character of a given practice. Let's say that I am learning to play the violin or basketball. I will listen to a great violin player (like David Oistrakh) or observe a great basketball player (like LeBron James) and seek to imitate them so that I may learn to play as well as they do, maybe even one day play better than they do. My comparisons and my striving can have two distinct goals (though often the two merge). My primary goal may be *to play well*, in which case I will compare my playing to theirs so as to learn and improve. My comparisons are in service of excellence; Oistrakh and James exemplify goals that may be possible to achieve and surpass and that are therefore reasonable to pursue.[49] Alternatively, my primary goal may be *playing better than they play*, in which case I will compare my playing to theirs so as to learn and, if I succeed, show that I am better than they are (which, in the two cases mentioned, would verge on being the greatest of all time). My comparisons are now in service of striving for superiority.

Second, the distinction between striving for superiority and striving for excellence is not that striving for superiority involves *competition,* whereas striving for excellence does not. Take two couplets of elite athletes who have competed with one another throughout their careers, as interpreted by Francisco Javier López Frías, a sports philosopher. In the rivalry between Lionel Messi and Cristiano Ronaldo, both players strived to outperform each other, breaking records and amassing titles, in a search for demonstrable and public superiority. In contrast, in the rivalry between Larry Bird and Magic Johnson, the focus was on mutual respect and admiration; both players have referred to their clashes as catalysts for self-improvement rather than as opportunities to achieve and demonstrate superiority.[50] Though striving for superiority always involves competition, relationships can be competitive without either party striving for superiority.[51]

A simple way to put the difference between striving for superiority and striving for excellence is to say that they have a distinct *object of desire.*[52] In striving for superiority, my goal is to stand above another person by a certain distance. In striving for excellence, my goal is to achieve some good, regardless of how I compare with others. The line between the two may be hard to draw in some cases, and both forms of striving can be pursued at the same time. One can engage in striving for excellence by striving for superiority (the Larry Bird and Magic Johnson rivalry, perhaps), and one can engage in striving for superiority by striving for excellence. Often enough, though, the distinction between the two is clear—and important, as I have suggested and will argue.

⚉

*Being better at something versus being better as a person.* One way to describe the general structure of striving for superiority is to use a triadic formula: "*A* strives to be superior to *B* at *C.*" *A* represents the one who is striving for superiority, *B* those over whom they are striving to be superior, and *C* the aspect in which they seek to be superior.[53] There are many *C*s in which we seek superiority, most of them some kind of performance or possession: how long we can hold our breath, how well we can play chess, or how virtuous we are; how great is our god, how big is our investment portfolio, or how well shaped are our toes. There is almost no limit to *C*s. The more important we, as a culture or group, tend to consider a *C*, the more important it will be to those belonging to the culture to be superior in *C* to others—if they embrace striving for superiority as a value.

Often, though, *A*'s superiority over *B* at *C* is taken as a sign of *A*'s more general superiority over *B*, that *A* is a better human being than *B*, a superior specimen of humanity. The obverse is, of course, that *B* is then worse as a human being, an inferior specimen of humanity. When striving for superiority concerns the *person*

21

rather than their "work," we have come to a key anthropological watershed. Do we all have equal worth as human beings independently of our performances or possessions, or is our worth as human beings dependent on our relative status as performers and possessors of qualities or things?

Stephen Darwall distinguishes between two kinds of respect.[54] One is appraisal-respect, which we show to people based on some performance or possession. Because people's performances and possessions differ, the appraisal-respect we accord them will differ too. The other kind of respect is recognition-respect, and we show it to human beings *as* human beings (or, for instance, to office holders by virtue of their office). All humans are equally human; they have equal worth as humans, and therefore the recognition-respect we owe them is equal.

Darwall builds on Immanuel Kant, who argues that our worth is based on our equal and common human "dignity," as distinguished from "worth" based on performance or possession. If we think that human beings have only worth and not dignity, then we will likely seek to strive for superiority, because superiority will increase any worth that we have as human beings. In contrast, if we think that human beings have dignity that requires equal recognition-respect, then in pursuing our own "worth" or in giving others appraisal-respect, we will have to be vigilant never to let better performances or greater possessions compromise the equality of recognition-respect.

Often, A strives to be better than B at C because A wants to be recognized as a better *person* than B. In fact, especially in our current social environments, superior performances and possessions tend to redound to the supposed superior worth of performers and possessors as human beings. The effect, and sometimes the intended goal, of the achieved superiority in performance or possession is to confer inferior worth on those who have been bested. We then have not only superior and inferior performances and possessions but also superior and inferior human beings.

22

The burden of such inferiority falls mainly on the "poor," those who are helpless and perceived as losers. Those who strive for superiority tend to disregard, exploit, or outright despise the poor, for helping them would not so much "disrupt the serenity of their happiness"[55] but interrupt their striving and set them back. As Jesus put it, those who strive to have the best seats in the houses of worship and places of honor at banquets are often the same as those who devour widows' houses (Mark 12:38–40). What Adela Cortina calls aporophobia, the rejection of the poor,[56] is particularly pronounced among those whose sense of self depends on being superior to others as human beings.

———※———

*Being superior versus being recognized as superior.*[57] Though closely related, we can distinguish between wanting to be better than someone and wanting others to acknowledge that we are better. Put differently, I may derive a certain satisfaction from *thinking myself* superior to other people, but often I take more satisfaction, or a different kind of satisfaction, in having *other people* acknowledge me as such. It is one thing for me to compare my car with that of my neighbor in my own head; it would be far worse to hear a couple of neighbors talking about those losers who don't have Audis or Teslas! Conversely, maybe I want to be a better violinist or soccer player than my rival, and maybe, in a sense, it would be enough for me to know that I am better than they are. But doubtless I would prefer for them—and a full concert hall or stadium—to acknowledge it too. As we saw earlier, Rousseau made that point a long time ago.

If the desire for superiority is nearly always also a desire to be recognized as superior, why does this distinction matter? One thing that we will see in the coming chapters is that, in environments where superiority becomes a key value, sometimes one's standing as superior in the public estimation—the *recognition* of one's superiority—can become detached and begin to float free from one's qualities or endowments, free from the things by which one can *be superior* in the first place, the Cs of the previous section. We might say that status or public ranking, then, becomes a good in its own right. One can strive for superior status without actually being better at anything. Conversely, one can be superior and have no desire to be recognized as such. Superiority and the recognition of superiority are therefore different. This difference accounts for the phenomenon of sheer status—superior or inferior—and will help to illuminate a number of examples in what follows.

=== ∭ ===

*Moral value versus instrumental value of striving for superiority.* Between 2008 and 2020, Lionel Messi was arguably the best player of the most popular sport in the world. Let's assume that he achieved that distinction by striving for superiority, say, in competition with a variety of rivals, including Cristiano Ronaldo, his career rival. If Messi's career was driven by striving for superiority, that striving helped him develop to near perfection a set of complex physical skills, which is a value in its own right, loosely comparable to virtuosic violin playing. It propelled him into fame, likely unmatched by any living human being at the peak of his glory. He is reported to have earned more than a billion dollars. Striving for superiority was of great instrumental value for him. My interest in this book is less with such instrumental value of striving for superiority than with its moral value, the moral good or evil that striving for superiority is for strivers and for those whom their striving affects.

## 6

One might wonder why I choose to focus on striving for superiority rather than some classical vice such as pride or envy that might be taken to motivate this kind of striving.[58] Or perhaps we should talk about how to cultivate the virtue of humility rather than introduce the new terminology of striving for superiority. Perhaps. I think, though, that there are good reasons why it is worth discussing striving for superiority in its own right. For one thing, I see striving for superiority as a pattern of human action and not simply as the vices with which it is associated or the virtues that we might cultivate to push against it. It is as a contagious behavior, enhanced by the modern logic of increase, that this sort of striving has become so ubiquitous in modern cultures.

Second, people may strive for superiority out of many motives, pride and envy among them. But people may also strive for superiority out of a sense of insecurity or inferiority. Or they may simply believe that striving for superiority is what one does, that striving to best others and possibly reach the status of the GOAT is what a life worth living looks like. If striving for superiority is about a specific object of desire, as I have defined it earlier, then I am interested here to explore whether it is in fact desirable. This is related to but not reducible to questions about particular virtues and vices.

Third, because striving for superiority is a behavior and not just an attitude, paying attention to it might help nudge us toward self-examination. Not many of us are likely to identify as proud or envious, or insofar as we do, we may be somewhat resigned to it, as a relatively stable feature of our disposition. But comparison and striving are ubiquitous features of modern life, and so talk of striving for superiority gives us specific behaviors and activities to consider (even if we decide that they are appropriate). In fact, as I will show in the coming chapters, it is possible to argue against striving for superiority even as one seeks to establish one's own intellectual or moral superiority by such an argument! The hope of this project, then, is to raise questions that may help us think more carefully about our moral lives—and new language is often helpful for provoking thought.

**7**

The critique of striving for superiority is feebly voiced today, barely audible. To make my case, I need allies. So, I sketch the problems of striving for superiority by exploring three Christian thinkers from different periods: a philosopher (Søren Kierkegaard), a poet (John Milton), and a theologian (Paul), as well as, more briefly, the teaching and example of Jesus and the account of Abraham and the people of Israel. In each exploration, partly distinct aspects of the problems of striving for superiority come into view as well—a distinct, though partly overlapping, alternative. But all my interlocutors, each in their own way and at times at odds with others, call striving for superiority into question. All support the main conviction of this book: that striving for superiority is bad, whether what we are striving to be superior at is itself good (like writing excellent poems) or deeply evil (like toppling the Most High).

What connects the first three figures is not just their critique of striving for superiority but the shaping influence on them of an ancient poem, or hymn, to Christ, the so-called Carmen Christi. The apostle Paul either composed it or incorporated it into his call to the members of the church in Philippi to relate to each other as if others were superior to them and to look out for the interests of others and not mainly their own (Phil. 2:3–4). The injunction in verse 5, "Let the same mind be in you that was in Christ Jesus," introduces the Carmen Christi, which then goes as follows:

> who, though he existed in the form of God,
>> did not regard equality with God
>> as something to be grasped,
> but emptied himself,
>> taking the form of a slave,
>> assuming human likeness.
> And being found in appearance as a human,
>> he humbled himself

and became obedient to the point of death—
even death on a cross.

Therefore God exalted him even more highly
and gave him the name
that is above every other name,
so that at the name given to Jesus
every knee should bend,
in heaven and on earth and under the earth,
and every tongue should confess
that Jesus Christ is Lord,
to the glory of God the Father. (2:6–11)

This hymn to Christ structures Milton's two great poems, *Paradise Lost* and *Paradise Regained*, and is key to his critique of Satan's ambition and to his account of the Son's victory over Satan.[59] Kierkegaard builds his critique of striving for superiority—what he calls the "restless mentality of comparison"[60]—mainly on the teaching of Christ. But the Carmen Christi is the lens through which he reads the coming into human flesh of the divine teacher, the God who "is not jealous for himself, but desires in love to be the equal of the humblest," as he puts it in *Philosophical Fragments*.[61] Since Kierkegaard and Milton draw on Paul and the Carmen Christi, why didn't I start the book with Paul rather than end it with his critique of striving for superiority and its alternative? Early in the project, I came to believe that Paul is not just more original but also more comprehensive and more compelling on the topic than either of the other two—or any other thinker I know, more comprehensive than anything we find in the teaching of Jesus or in the Hebrew Bible. Still, the last word belongs to Jesus and to the calling of the people of Israel.

A narrow range of interlocutors—most are central figures of Western Christianity, all are males and born before the beginning of the twentieth century—is a limitation of this book. It is largely a feature of the accidents of my physical and intellectual biography, and it diminishes the comprehensiveness and, for some, the persuasiveness—though I hope not the truthfulness—of my exploration. But that very limitation is also an invitation to others to take up the topic with different interlocutors—and contest, confirm, or refine what I offer here. My central aim is to reignite a vigorous and rigorous conversation about what I consider to be one of the most important of the neglected topics concerning life in contemporary cultures of modernity.

# 2

# The Worry of Comparison (Kierkegaard)

Søren Kierkegaard's most memorable take on why striving for superiority is a problem comes in the form of a parable. He tells it as he discusses Jesus's teaching about worry in the Sermon on the Mount. "Therefore I tell you, do not worry about your life, what you will eat or what you will drink, or about your body, what you will wear" (Matt. 6:25), Jesus says to the crowd gathered in a field under an open sky. "Therefore" links the commandment to the previous verse, where Jesus teaches, "No one can serve two masters, for a slave will either hate the one and love the other or be devoted to the one and despise the other. You cannot serve God and wealth" (6:24). Worry is a symptom that one serves the false god Mammon—that is, wealth—or some other false god, like power or, encompassing both wealth and power, distinction. To illustrate why his listeners should not worry, Jesus invites them to consider the birds of the sky and the lilies of the field. God feeds the birds and clothes the lilies without the help of their worry.

29

Most in Jesus's audience led precarious lives, living day to day. The petition in the Lord's Prayer "give us today our *daily* bread" reflects that reality. They could not be certain whether their most basic needs for food and shelter would be met the next day. Expanding Jesus's teaching about worry to include those whose survival needs *are* met, Kierkegaard zeroes in on the worry about *distinctions* in how those needs are met. Writing as Copenhagen's economy finally recovered decades after the British had almost completely destroyed the city in 1807, Kierkegaard was very much aware of the precarity of life. He himself lived from inherited wealth, however. Like most readers of this book (but unlike many in the world today), he did not have to worry about basic necessities. For him, Jesus's teaching about worry is mainly about what we *think* we should eat and wear so as not to experience ourselves as inferior to our neighbors or so as not to have our sense of superiority compromised. This is what he calls "the worry of comparison."[1] Human needs, even such basic needs as those for food and clothing, he thinks, are not mere psychic echoes of the threats to our precarious bodiliness. They are largely attuned to social expectations. Leaving the problem of precarity to the side—not entirely dismissing it, just not taking it up—Kierkegaard explores the worry to which striving for distinction gives rise.

To illustrate his main point, in *Upbuilding Discourses in Various Spirits* (1847), Kierkegaard tells a parable of a field lily. Here is a very brief version. A very contented little lily is growing among other flowers near a brook. To a person with eyes to see, it is clothed more gloriously than Solomon ever was, the most glamorous king who ever ruled. One day, a little bird comes and visits the lily, befriends it, and tells it of gorgeous, glorious lilies the bird saw growing elsewhere as she was roaming in the sky. The bird is naughty, writes Kierkegaard. Instead of delighting in the loveliness of the lily, she shows off her superior knowledge ascertained on account of her ability to move around freely. Worse, she "usually ended her story with the comment, humiliating to the lily, that in comparison

30

with that kind of glory the lily looked like nothing—indeed, it was so insignificant that it was a question whether the lily actually had a right to be called a lily." The little lily feels inferior not just to those gorgeous lilies but to the bird that can fly as well. Naturally, it begins to worry, "to be preoccupied with itself and the condition of its life—all day long." The worry gives birth to a consuming craving to become itself "a gorgeous lily in the company of all others, or perhaps even a Crown Imperial, envied by all others."[2] It is not hard to guess how the story ends. To satisfy the lily's craving, the little bird agrees to peck the ground around the lily, carefully uproot it, and carry it to the place where, in the company of gorgeous lilies, it can fulfill its dream of being the envy of everyone. On the way to the land of its aspired glory, the worried lily withers and dies. Fleeing from inferiority by striving for superiority kills her.

## 1

Comparisons and striving for superiority presuppose diversity. Kierkegaard is keenly aware of differences among humans, and he celebrates them. An important goal of his whole philosophy is to rescue unique individuals from the leveling effects of the "crowd" and, more broadly, of the *Zeitgeist*, from being swallowed either by totality (as in the philosophy of his great nemesis Georg W. F. Hegel) or by some impersonal world historical process (as in the social theory of Karl Marx).[3] Each human being is distinct from and dissimilar to all others.

> No person has ever lived in Christendom, any more than in paganism, who is not dressed or cloaked in the dissimilarity of earthly life. Just as little as the Christian lives or can live without his body, so little can he live without the dissimilarity of earthly life that belongs to every human being in particular by birth, by position, by circumstances, by education, etc.—none of us is pure humanity.[4]

Kierkegaard's "dissimilarity" is broader than our "diversity." Covering more than categories like class, race, gender, and ethnicity, it refers to anything that sets individual humans apart from one another, like contrasting friend versus foe, kin versus stranger, learned versus uneducated, eminent versus lowly, and so on. Kierkegaard thinks that each person is equally and unalterably just as much human as any other and that each is so in their own specific way, that each is necessarily, though partly alterably, "cloaked in the dissimilarity of earthly life." Christianity has no interest in stripping humans of differences. Far from wanting to create some generic pure humanity, its goal is "only to make humans pure"—with all their differences.[5]

Although we can never encounter humanity in pure form, in Kierkegaard's view, differences among humans do not define their humanity. If they did, the possibility would open of considering some humans, those whose differences are unimpressive, to be less human or not human at all. This is the mistake made by the lily, which, under the bird's influence, started thinking itself so insignificant that it no longer had the right to be called a lily.[6] Such dehumanization, Kierkegaard thinks, is a danger in paganism, which, in his view, has no resources for—and perhaps no interest in—affirming the equal humanity and kinship of all humans.[7] In Christianity, he argues, more central than differences is the common humanity of all. The gospel message, after all, is addressed to each of us as a mere human being: one whom God has made and Jesus Christ has redeemed.[8] Humans go catastrophically wrong when they center their lives in "temporal dissimilarities of the worldly" rather than in God, and when they therefore forget that every human being, without exception, is to be as honored and loved as any other. Though each is to be loved "individually," no one is to be loved "exceptionally."[9]

Kierkegaard's stance on striving for superiority is tied to his stress on the primacy of the love of neighbor—unconditional yet individuated love of any person by virtue of their humanity—over erotic love and friendship love. Both these loves are preferential and dependent on the specific characteristics of the objects of love. This makes them forms of self-love, Kierkegaard argues.[10] As long as the lily was alone, it was safe. When the naughty bird made the lily imagine itself in the company of others, it entered a danger zone. Unlike lilies, humans are intrinsically social, and much of what is best about humanity arises out of our sociality. But the company of distinct and differing human beings is a major source of temptation as well, a point that was central to Rousseau, as I showed in chapter 1.[11] "In daily association with people, in the multifarious diversity and its various connections, one forgets . . . what it is to be a human being, forgets it because of the diversity among individuals."[12] Comparisons and, specifically, as I will shortly explain, their restlessness generate such amnesia. A little lily compares itself to others, forgets its own intrinsic glory, strains to fend off the anguish of perceived inferiority, strives for superiority—and withers.

═══ ⅲ ═══

As I noted in chapter 1, many people in modern societies believe that striving for superiority is just what humans do. Such striving is necessary for survival and key to human progress. Friedrich Nietzsche, a fierce critic of modernity, argues that striving for superiority—a *certain kind* of it, as he sees it—not only fosters excellence but also provides a much better substitute for life-denying moralities, whether religious or philosophical. In contrast, Kierkegaard argues that striving for superiority undermines our very humanity. There is a danger that, in the process of comparing, we will latch on to our differences and distinctions while still thinking that our qualities and achievements can be directly compared—and in all this forget our common humanity. This way of being in the world Kierkegaard calls "the restless mentality of comparison." The person who has succumbed to this mentality "finally goes so far that because of diversity he forgets that he is a human being, in despair regards himself as so different from other people that he even regards himself as different from what it is to be human."[13] The source of the problem is not differences or sociality as such but a particular attitude of the individual toward them.

Let's start with Kierkegaard's analysis of comparison in general before coming to the question of what might make comparison restless. When there is nobody with whom to compare oneself either in real life or in imagination, comparisons are, obviously, impossible. When others are around, comparisons are inevitable, Kierkegaard thinks. Comparisons are implicit even in conversing with others; in merely *looking at* others, we tend to compare. Commenting on Job's comforters, who sat with their greatly afflicted friend in silence for seven days, Kierkegaard writes, "No individual can be present, even though in silence, in such a way that his presence means nothing by the way of comparison."[14]

As they all sit together in stillness, both Job and his comforters are comparing. They are comparing his current state of affliction with his former state of great prosperity, deep piety, and high repute. They are also comparing his status to the status of his friends. He was "the greatest of all the people of the East" (Job 1:3)—and they looked up to him, perhaps reluctantly and with some envy. Now Job's greatness has crumbled, and they tower above him. He is sitting in the ashes bereft of all but his troubled life, and their lot has remained unchanged. These are all simple comparisons, but one can sense how easily they can become what Kierkegaard calls "restless" and turn into competitive claims of superiority and inferiority. The seeds of striving for superiority are already in the comparisons. I will show a similar dynamic in Milton's account of the human fall in the book of Genesis: Eve starts with innocent comparing and, misled by the "naughty bird" called Satan, ends up striving to be the best in all creation (see chap. 3 below).

The gap between better and worse makes it possible for comparisons to become *restless* and competitive. The explicit aim of competition is often no more than equality—elevation from the state of inferiority. But since every human is unique, what Kierkegaard calls "temporal dissimilarities of the worldly"[15] cannot be eliminated, and strict equality can never be achieved. As beings in space and time, all humans are distinct from one another, and within the frame of worldliness, without appeal to God, the Creator and lover of creatures, there is no measure according to which they can be deemed equal.[16] And even if equality could be achieved, it can never remain stable and secure. As a result, even in desiring not to be worse off than others, each tends to want to be at least slightly better than others. Deceived by "smiling vanity," in comparing themselves to others, each desires to "be the ruler," to "be a prodigy."[17]

As Job's friends sit and observe him, honoring his suffering in silence, they don't just think that they are better off than Job. Believing that the law of the harvest—you reap what you have sown—is the moral order of the universe, they think that they prosper because they are righteous and that Job suffers because he has sinned. They consider themselves not just better off than Job but morally superior to him. When they address Job after his first desperate speech, in which he curses the day on which he was born, they flaunt their superiority under the guise of friendly advice. In the process, they unwittingly bear witness to the inadequacy, even inhumanity, of meritocratic thinking (which Paul emphasizes as well, as I will show in chaps. 4 and 5).

This is the restless mentality of comparison, whether it comes in meritocratic or non-meritocratic forms. Later in *Upbuilding Discourses*, Kierkegaard describes it as "craving for distinction by way of comparison."[18] The craving for superiority can be modest, in which we desire "to have at least one human being to rule over"[19]—"rule" here being used in the broad sense of "being better than" someone. But craving for superiority can also be proud and vain, even narcissistic, in which case we desire to "rule" over everyone, to be and to be seen as supreme, the greatest of all time.

## 2

One might think that engaging in restless comparisons born out of striving for superiority is simply what it means to be a grown-up human rather than an innocent child. Kierkegaard disagrees. Restless comparisons damage the soul, and they do this regardless of whether a person groans under a sense of inferiority or basks in superiority. At one point, Kierkegaard describes striving for superiority as "one of the most corrupting kinds of defilement."[20] Why so?

First, there is the *affliction of worry*, as I have already shown. Whether we are low or high on the scale of comparative distinctions, we worry. If we are low, we worry about how to rise to the level of our neighbors and above. If we are high, we worry about being overtaken. Wherever on the scale we are, there are almost always people below and above us, and so we worry in both directions. When we see ourselves as better than others, we become arrogant on account of our superiority and despise those who are worse; when we see ourselves as worse than others, we envy and groan under the weight of our inferiority. Either way, we worry.

Second, restless comparisons—as distinct from those in which we only note differences—tend to *erase the particular character of each person*; they are inherently untruthful. When we compare ourselves, we are putting ourselves in someone else's place or putting someone else in our place.[21] Restless, competitive comparisons measure each person by their success in acquiring certain goods deemed valuable—intellectual prowess, moral rectitude, wealth, beauty, and so on—and rank them on a scale from low to high, from worst to best. In the social space that comparisons create, success or failure according to those scales becomes the defining feature of each person. That they may be beautiful in a different way—according to other criteria of beauty—or that they may have other kinds of intelligence is disregarded. We also tend to disregard other features that make up their character. Scales flatten what is unique into something common.

Third, Kierkegaard notes that assessing a person using a common scale to determine their standing *undermines their sense of self*: "In his contacts with others [i.e., other human beings] it seems as if at every moment he must wait in order to find out from the others what he is now at this moment."[22] A person is dispersed into myriads of moving images, each acquired in comparison with a particular person at a given time. They are always waiting to know who they are as each moment a new self, acquired in each fresh comparison, replaces the old.

Fourth, restless comparisons *devalue the incomparable glory of* what Kierkegaard calls *mere humanity*. In the Sermon on the Mount, Jesus claims that even Solomon in all his glory was not clothed as beautifully as an ordinary field lily. Kierkegaard reasons that if any lily is more glorious than Solomon's royal splendor, the same must be even more true of any human being. All of Solomon's glory as a king "is nothing in comparison with what every human being is by being human, so that in order to be the most glorious thing he is and to be conscious of this Solomon must strip off all his glory and just be a human being!"[23] Our very humanity is a much greater good than any distinctions among us, a point toward which Milton gestures in writing about the "naked majesty" of Adam and Eve in paradise (*Paradise Lost* 4:290; see chap. 3). This is the heart of Kierkegaard's case against striving for superiority. To understand what he is after, I need to make a brief foray into his anthropology.

═══ ▦ ═══

Because human beings are self-conscious, we can "step out" of ourselves and relate ourselves to ourselves. The self, Kierkegaard claims, is that relation between me and myself. But human beings are never alone, self-standing and self-established. I always need another; I relate myself to myself by relating to another. In the opening pages of *The Sickness unto Death*, written shortly after the texts about restless comparisons I examined earlier, Kierkegaard defines the self as "a relation that relates itself to itself and in relating itself to itself *relates itself to another*."[24] So far I have noted two relations: the self to itself and the self to another self. But such a self, a self-relating and other-relating self, cannot exist, states Kierkegaard, without a third relation, and that is God's constitutive—creative—relation to just such a self. The self is established by the infinite and eternal God, and the self lives and does everything it does, whether consciously or unconsciously, in relation to God, *before* God—that very "power that established it."[25]

Since a self is a relation, this opens the possibility of misrelations. Kierkegaard thinks that we can betray our humanity in the way we relate to ourselves and to others. This is the point of the book's title: *The Sickness unto Death*. He is referring not to physical death but to spiritual death, the death of the true self. His other designation for such death is despair—despair not as an emotional state, as we tend to think of it, but as the falsehood of the self, the state of its self-betrayal, which is "not only the worst misfortune and misery" but the self's "ruination."[26]

To understand why this sickness is so bad, we need to know what health is. Describing genuine health, Kierkegaard writes, "The formula that describes the state of the self when despair is completely rooted out is this: in relating itself to itself and in willing to be itself, the self rests transparently in the power that established it."[27] In this quote, "the power that established" the self is God. To rest transparently means to be at one with ourselves in relationship to another— the way we are at one with ourselves when we are engrossed in music or when we are in the flow while working on something we love. We are healthy, Kierkegaard states, when we are willing to be ourselves by being at one with ourselves in relationship with the God in whom we have our being and before whom we live.

There are two chief forms of despair. One is "not to will to be oneself." That is how we might ordinarily think of despair. The other form of despair is surprising and is key to our exploration of striving for superiority. This despair is "to will to be oneself" but to do so *primarily through relating to others who are not God*. That is where worldly distinctions and restless comparisons come in.

— ⅲ —

When I relate to myself primarily through relating to other people in the social space defined by ranked distinctions and striving for superiority, when I seek to establish myself through wealth, power, education, ethnic belonging, and such, and when I do so in a competitive way, striving to be as good as or better than others, I am in a state of despair. I am no longer transparent, no longer at rest in being at one with myself. I am divided between self-deprecation and striving for glory and superiority. The competitive striving that shapes my relationships to others poisons and destabilizes my relationship to myself. The image of myself that I create in the likeness of other humans—like the beautiful little lily imagining itself as a Crown Imperial—occludes my own unique and glorious humanity. When I seek to create myself in the image of the best worldly specimens, they take the place of God and I ruin myself. I "die" as I am taken by the naughty bird away from being the person God established me to be to what I, in restless comparisons with others, mistakenly aspire to be. Of course, being at one with oneself in God is not a passive state but a dynamic relation. It is the result of actively receiving oneself as always already established by God as a distinct person in relation to oneself and others on a journey through time.

Every human being, each in their own way, has the same glory, and this glory is incomparably greater than the glory of any distinction they could struggle themselves into. As a mountaineer standing on top of a high mountain surveys the play of clouds' shapes below, so every human, just by being human, stands on the highest peak and observes all the diversity of humanity without envy or pride.[28] Striving for superiority turns a glorious being into an insubstantial cloud, Kierkegaard implies. In *Christian Discourses*, he puts it this way: in their innermost being, such a person is as good as dead; it is rather only their loftiness, and not their true self, that walks among us—only a shell of a true human being, an insubstantial ghost.[29] In striving for superiority, the self is lost. Both its common humanity and its unique particularity are betrayed.

What is the goal for which human beings burden themselves with the affliction of worry and fall into a state of alienation from themselves? It is superiority or, in Kierkegaard's terms, "loftiness." But loftiness is a fiction. Now, the properties for which we are striving—say, a certain muscle tone, a quality of prose, capaciousness of memory, and so on—need not be a fiction (though some clearly are, like having the longest beard in the world) and may even be genuinely desirable. But the sense of superiority over another person ("loftiness") on account of that property is fictitious, Kierkegaard claims.

Let's say one strives after a certain kind of beauty—as did the worried little lily, or as did a little black girl named Pecola in Toni Morrison's *The Bluest Eye*. Pecola desperately wanted blue eyes because both the contempt of the racialized gaze and the glamour of white stardom had made her imagine blue eyes as the pinnacle of beauty. Now, a Crown Imperial lily may indeed be beautiful, and blue eyes too. But to take that particular form of beauty as the dominant and universal norm is to turn it into a dehumanizing fiction. Persons craving distinction with regard to such ideals of beauty mostly lose the battle for loftiness, and they end up losing themselves, even dying, in chasing after falsehood—as both the worried lily and the racially self-loathing Pecola did.[30]

The fate of the winners is better, but in Kierkegaard's view, not by much. Describing a man "hankering after loftiness" expressed in titles, he writes,

He has himself become what was coveted: a title regarded as a human being. Within [that human being] there is sheer emptiness and trumpery—indeed, there is nothing. But the appearance is there, the vain appearance that bears the marks of worldly lofti- ness that command the deference of the passerby—while he bears all this loftiness somewhat as the cushions that bear his medals at the funeral.[31]

As I will show in chapter 4, the apostle Paul also exposes the "weak- ness" and "lack of honor" of some members as mere appearances —though appearances that are powerful enough to ruin community and that members of the community must therefore relinquish.

## 3

What is Kierkegaard's alternative to sliding into nothingness by striving for superiority? Seeking to eliminate "worldly dissimilari- ties," on which striving for superiority depends, is not an option. Dissimilarities are not only valuable; they are also ineliminable. Our common humanity exists only in as many dissimilar exem- plars as there are humans. We can eliminate dissimilarities only by eliminating humans.

Another option would be to maximize similarities while know- ing that it is impossible to achieve a full and stable sameness of equality. But that, too, would involve significant erasure of par- ticularities. More importantly, mere similarities would not get closer to where Kierkegaard thinks we need to be. The craving for distinction by way of comparison would remain, even if the gap between the lowly and the lofty was greatly reduced. As Georg Simmel observes, social emotions attach themselves not so much to absolute differences as to relative ones. He illustrates the point with the parable "Roses." Imagine a land full of successful farmers, some of whom grow useful and healthy food, others of whom grow the most beautiful roses imaginable. We tend to understand why tensions and jealousy should arise between the two sorts of farm- ers, why those who grow roses only for their beauty might regard themselves as superior, and why those who grow food would rebel against them. But even if a regime of rose farmers, all equal in wealth, were to be established, soon the same jealousy and pride and the same sense of inferiority and superiority would arise on account of "the smallest differences in color and form, in smell and charm with which nature resists all attempts at uniformity."[32]

———※———

Kierkegaard's bold and controversial proposal is that we should give up on craving for distinction by way of comparisons and eliminate both the worry about being inferior and the striving to be superior.[33] Though each person is part of a vast network of dissimilarities, "all this . . . comparing dissimilarity does not preoccupy Christianity at all, not in the least—such a preoccupation and concern is again nothing but worldliness."[34]

Our teachers should be the lilies and the birds—not the naughty, seducing birds, like the one who ruined the little lily, but the good ones, as Jesus taught, who do not worry but are still fed by God (Matt. 6:26). Here is how Kierkegaard puts it in *Christian Discourses*: though there are levels of eminence between a sparrow and a goldfinch, such a classification does not exist for them. Each "is what it is" and is "contented with itself"; it does not worry "whether it is 'just as good a bird' as the others. . . . Of all such things it does not think at all, so impatient it is in its joy of being."[35] Of course, humans are not birds. We are thinking creatures, aware of the distinction between lowly and eminent. Still, the goal is to be like a sparrow: impatient in the joy of being ourselves.

The goal is also to be like a lily, living "in its innocent self-satisfaction" without the "least little trace of the care of lowliness."[36] It is free not just of the care of lowliness but also of the sense of self-importance on account of its extraordinary beauty. In an earlier use of the metaphor of the lily, which God arrayed in a garb more glorious than that of Solomon, Kierkegaard asks rhetorically,

Would it not be a sorry delusion of the lily's, if when it looked upon its fine raiment it thought that it was on account of that raiment that the God loved it? Instead of standing dauntless in the field, sporting with the wind, carefree as the gust that blows, would it not under the influence of such a thought languish and droop, not daring to lift up its head?[37]

If the lily thought so, it would become plagued by the care of loftiness, by the sense that it is not lofty if "it is not *loftier* than others."[38]

But how can a human being come to live without the care of lowliness or loftiness? One might think that identifying how one is different from anyone else is a good start: one identifies consciously one's particularity and rests in it with self-satisfaction. But Kierkegaard argues that this simple and seemingly obvious procedure is a snare. The endeavor involves comparisons and is therefore likely to end up in striving for superiority and thereby in a ghostlike nothingness. What is required for humans to acquire the joy of being and innocent self-satisfaction is to shift the object of our self-evaluations. Only by focusing on our mere humanity rather than on our distinctions can we come to rest "transparently in the power that established" us.[39] We need to recognize ourselves as living "before God"—*coram Deo*—with the God of love as the primary reference for our identities.

For Kierkegaard, "humanity" is not something that a person achieves.[40] If it were, it would invite comparisons; we could be more or less human. And it would not be able to get us out of worry of comparison and into the joy of being. Instead, "humanity" is given to each of us simply by being particular human creatures. As to conformity to Christ, the prototype, this does come in degrees, but success in conformity is not an achievement of the individual either, even if there is a kind of striving involved. The prototype is not a mere example but also a reliable promise; "no other promise is so reliable," Kierkegaard insists, because "the prototype is indeed the fulfillment."[41] Each person's unique growth in resemblance to the prototype is thus also a gift. To use the vocabulary of Paul, to whom I will turn in chapter 4, each person's true self is the self that is constituted by Christ living in them. Living before God, I don't accrue credit or merit, and therefore I cannot justifiably think of myself as superior or inferior to anyone else.[42] As to any other particular feature of a particular human being—their aesthetic qualities, intellectual abilities, wealth, or social power—their value rests entirely on the extent to which these features are modes of living in resemblance to the prototype.

There is only one genuine loftiness, one true earthly glory: a human being living *coram Deo* in response to God's call and resting transparently in God. Each is lofty in this way, writes Kierkegaard, "without being higher than anyone else"[43]—and without needing to worry at all about how high or low in worldly terms they are. Each lives out the joy of their own being irrespective of their relative status among others. That applies to any human, even those considered to be the loftiest. To be truly lofty, the loftiest of all royals, for instance, must live "above the difference of loftiness." Lofty in this way, a royal will be exactly equal to their lowliest subject, who has also come to live "above the difference of lowliness."[44] Any status that is deemed lofty in worldly terms is in fact lowly, mere clouds, each perhaps beautiful in its own way, beneath the mountaintop of the glorious "mere" humanity. On that loftiest mountaintop, mere humans are surrounded by their teachers, the birds of the air and the flowers of the field, and all other creatures, each one of which God establishes and loves equally.

## 4

Kierkegaard contrasts the self-satisfaction of loftiness before God with the paradoxical self-undermining of striving for superiority. "Self-satisfaction" is an ambiguous term, though. He distinguishes between "innocent" and "proud" self-satisfaction as well as between what we might call "aspiring" and "indifferent" self-satisfaction.

Kierkegaard uses the phrase "innocent self-satisfaction" as a near synonym to the "joy of being." His example is a bird in the company of other birds, whose "joy lives freely in the alternating of voices" with other birds. Though each is gratified to sing in chorus with the others, it "does not sing to gratify the others." It does not need their approval or, even less, a sense of superiority over them to be "satisfied with being itself."[45] This contrasts with a kind of self-satisfaction rooted in prideful comparisons. In the Gospel of Luke, Jesus tells a parable about those "who trusted in themselves that they were righteous and regarded others with contempt" (18:9). In the parable, a Pharisee is the anti-type of those birds. He needs to think of himself as superior to others to be satisfied with himself. In thanking God that he is "not like other people: thieves, rogues, adulterers, or even like this tax collector" (18:11), he, Kierkegaard notes, "proudly found self-satisfaction in seeing the tax collector" and in "measuring the distance from" him and from others like him.[46] As the Pharisee celebrates his superiority before God, his self-satisfaction shows itself as arrogant contempt.[47]

Kierkegaard's favorite designation for "innocent self-satisfaction" and for the "joy of being" is "contentment."[48] To be contented generally means to be satisfied with oneself as one is, to be disinterested in improving oneself or one's condition. Like a sparrow or a lily, contented people simply are what they are. But that's not exactly what Kierkegaard means by contentment. Since growing in conformity to the prototype (Christ) is central to his project, the kind of contentment he has in mind must also be compatible with improvement of the very self that is satisfied with itself. It must be an *aspiring* rather than an indifferent kind of self-contentment. As he puts it in some of the discarded material from *The Sickness unto Death*, "It would indeed be blasphemous to praise the ideal and not strive after it oneself."[49]

Kierkegaard's account of admiration illustrates well how he combines self-satisfaction and self-improvement. He encourages admiration even though it involves comparing oneself with someone, affirming their superiority (in a certain domain), and striving to be like them. There is a difference, though, between restless comparisons, with their striving for superiority, and admiring comparisons combined with self-contentment.

There are two ways in which we can admire another person: one involving painful self-deprecation and the other joyful self-delight. In a passage taken from his discussion of strength and weakness in *Christian Discourses*, Kierkegaard spells out what it means to admire without the pain of feeling one's inferiority.

> Admiration . . . can be seen from two sides. . . . Its first side is a feeling of weakness when the admiring one relates himself in admiration to superiority. But admiration is a happy relation to superiority, and therefore it is a blessed feeling; in true unanimity with oneself, it is perhaps more blessed to admire than to be the one admired. That admiration's first feeling is one of pain is seen in this, that if someone senses superiority but admits it reluctantly, not joyfully, then he is far from being happy: on the contrary he is exceedingly unhappy, in the most distressing pain. But as soon as he yields to the superiority that he still basically but unhappily admired, and yields in admiration, then the joy of this is victorious in him. The more surrendered he is, the more unanimous with himself in admiring, the closer he is to almost becoming superior to the superiority. In his admiration he is indescribably happily freed from every pressure of superiority; he does not succumb to the superiority, but he is victorious in admiration.[50]

If I admire a person who is courageous in a way that I feel I could never be and do so with a sense of pained inferiority, I am admiring them in the wrong way. In fact, Kierkegaard thinks that I am not admiring them at all, for genuine admiration is "a blessed feeling," "a happy relation to superiority." Still, that happy relation is not a detached amazement, a passive admiration. One should be not a mere admirer but an imitator. Explaining the difference, Kierkegaard writes, "An imitator *is* or strives *to be* what he admires, and an admirer keeps himself personally detached, consciously or unconsciously does not discover that what is admired involves a claim upon him, to be or at least to strive to be what is admired."[51] When I genuinely admire someone with courage superior to my own, I affirm it as admirable, I rejoice to see it instantiated in the world, and I desire to possess it myself *in my own way*. I do not envy them; I neither feel diminished in their presence nor strive to achieve superiority over them. I strive for courage like theirs, not to keep up with *them* or exceed *them* but to become a better version of myself in becoming like them. In admiring them, I am unanimous with myself.

In an important sense, such happy admiration, Kierkegaard notes, might be "superior" to the superiority of the one we admire—in a sense, akin to the greater loftiness of being human than being a royal. I have conquered the temptation of striving for superiority and am on the mountaintop of the glory of my particular form of mere humanity, diligently stretching myself into my own fullness—and all this while observing those superior to me with admiration and joy. This is "innocent self-satisfaction" in the process of growth into fullness. It stands in sharp contrast to "proud self-satisfaction," the obverse of which is the unhappy relation to superiority.

———— ⫯⫯⫯ ————

Striving to embody the qualities we admire—those supremely exemplified in Christ as the prototype—is just one category of work that the properly self-satisfied, contented human being willing to be oneself does. Work more generally is a human perfection for Kierkegaard. "By working, human beings resemble God, who indeed also works"; if they work well, in fact, they work "together with God."[52] Those who have overcome the "wretchedness of worldly comparisons" and who know what true honor and per-fection are also know "how glorious it is to work"[53]—in a similar way as it is glorious to be human. The purpose of work is not to satisfy the craving for distinction by comparison but to imitate the prototype, to serve others, and thereby to live more fully into the personal distinctiveness that comes with being established in one's humanity by God. Striving after things like a job in which we may exercise our calling is what we can and should be after. Kierkegaard would urge, though, that in whatever position we find ourselves and whatever our distinctiveness may be, we should "wear" them loosely. What matters more than any particular form of our distinctiveness is the "mere humanity" of our concrete life and its "transparency" to God.[54]

## 5

As I have presented him, Kierkegaard seems disinterested in the moral salience of the differences in the conditions of life of the lowly and the lofty. His concern is the *worry* of poverty, the *worry* of abundance, and the *worry* of comparisons, not the *conditions* of poverty, the *conditions* of abundance, and the *conditions* that make restless comparisons difficult to avoid. Distinctions in condi-tions seem not to count in his thinking about striving for superior-ity. The lofty and the lowly in worldly relations (*coram mundo*) are equally lowly when it comes to the only loftiness that counts—namely, living our worldly lives with one another in joyous and diligent contentment before God (*coram Deo*).

Kierkegaard even argues that the poor and weak have an advan-tage over the rich and powerful just because of their poverty and weakness. Since they are not surrounded and propped up by wealth and power that lead them to glory in their distinction, the poor can more easily recognize the emptiness of worldly loftiness. He thinks, not entirely plausibly, that the poor will also find it easier to give up striving for worldly loftiness and thus be more likely to set themselves on the journey to true loftiness. This advantage of the lowly is not in itself a moral one; it is an advantage of being exempt from certain powerful temptations. Conversely, a lofty person, in a worldly sense, is here at a disadvantage. But those who are lofty in the worldly sense have no excuse, for they can help themselves "by literally becoming poor, scorned, lowly";[55] they can remove themselves from the circumstances of temptation. Still, decisive in both cases are not their exterior conditions but rather the internal attitude, "a feeling of one's own lowliness," irrespective of worldly status.[56] And the feeling of genuine human loftiness that all humans share.

(The idea that the lowly are at a moral advantage over the lofty when it comes to their ability to resist the temptation to strive for superiority has *some* plausibility in premodern, static societies in which the gap between the rich and the poor was thought to be [almost] unbridgeable because mobility was structurally limited. It is less plausible in modern, dynamic societies, especially those in which rags-to-riches stories are part of the social ideology. In such societies, striving for superiority in competition with others is often a condition of survival for the lowly. If so, taking seriously the problem of striving for superiority might require kinds of social policy that would not require cutthroat competition among the poor.)

———— ⚬ ————

The *feeling* of one's own lowliness is essential for Kierkegaard, but so is *acting* in the world in light of our relation to God and common humanity. What are the consequences of our common lowliness before God on the relation of the lofty toward the lowly (in the worldly sense)? Kierkegaard does not explore this question extensively, but what he does say is important.

In the Gospel of Luke, Jesus tells the host who invited him to his place,

> When you give a luncheon or a dinner, do not invite your friends or your brothers and sisters or your relatives or rich neighbors, in case

they may invite you in return, and you would be repaid. But when you give a banquet, invite the poor, the crippled, the lame, and the blind. And you will be blessed because they cannot repay you, for you will be repaid at the resurrection of the righteous. (14:12–14)

The obvious question, which is at the center of the instruction, is, Why invite the poor? The response Jesus gives is, "Because they cannot repay you" (14:14). The invitation to the poor is an act of love, not a clandestine barter, "repayment" at the resurrection of the righteous notwithstanding. In *Works of Love*, Kierkegaard explores a less obvious question about the story: Why does Jesus call the meal for the rich relatives and friends "a luncheon" or "a dinner," whereas the one for the disadvantaged he calls "a banquet"? Would not a more appropriate designation be "a charity meal"? It might seem that a meal for the lowly cannot be a banquet, even if the food is "choice and costly" and even if there are "ten kinds of wine."[57] Without friends and select company, how can there be a banquet? Still, Jesus insists on changing the cultural practice and its designation: "inviting the poor—that is giving a banquet." Kierkegaard continues: "So scrupulous is Christian equality and its use of language that it requires not only that you shall feed the poor; it requires that you shall call it a banquet."[58] But why?

Given dissimilarities between the lofty and the lowly, this *preference* for the lowly—the preferential option for the poor!—is what it means to love one's neighbors without reference to either their lowlines or your loftiness: "each individually but no one exceptionally."[59] With no concern for the effects of the deed on your own social standing, elevate the lowly to the status of equality with the lofty; don't treat "the poor and the lowly only as the poor and the lowly."[60]

=== ‡ ===

Such banquets for the poor notwithstanding, the dissimilarities, including discrepancies in wealth, power, or social standing, are to remain, according to Kierkegaard. One reason is his static view of society: since God's providence allots dissimilarities, each person should accept their dissimilarities and remain in their "proper place."[61] The other reason is his conviction that any human endeavor to scatter "the proud in the imagination of their hearts," to bring "down the powerful from their thrones and [lift] up the lowly" (Luke 1:51–52) involves struggle, reinforces divisions, and makes it impossible to see what is most important: the equal inner glory of each person. Christianity, writes Kierkegaard,

> has not wanted to storm forth to abolish dissimilarity, neither the dissimilarity of distinction nor of lowliness; nor has it wished to effect in a worldly way a worldly compromise among the dissimilarities; but it wants the dissimilarity to hang loosely on the individual, as loosely as the cape the king casts off in order to show who he is, as loosely as the ragged costume in which a supranatural being has disguised himself.[62]

Instead of abolishing social dissimilarities, Kierkegaard advises, we should resist craving for distinction by way of comparison, which reinforces dissimilarities; we should seek to grow away from worrying about dissimilarities and into seeing through them the all-important glory of the "mere" humanity of each, the equal glory of the lowliest and the loftiest.

We may grant Kierkegaard's point that it is impossible to conquer the craving for superiority by changing the conditions of the world. Distinctions onto which restless comparisons can latch are ineliminable, as Simmel's parable "Roses" illustrates. But it seems that Kierkegaard could not object to struggling, for instance, against the cultural dominance of the ideal of blue eyes, which costs Pecola her life. An astute social psychologist, Kierkegaard would be the first to insist that cultures can be marked by particular vices that shape concrete social patterns.[63] While Kierkegaard perhaps tended to emphasize that changing social conditions will not make people intrinsically more virtuous, that did not keep him from naming what he saw as the determining vices of his culture.

We can thus love each human sacrificially and no one exceptionally while at the same time protesting against the cultural dominance of certain ideals and the striving for superiority associated with them. If we can ask the lofty to let their dissimilarities hang loosely, as Kierkegaard does, we can, by the same token, work for cultural change. We can collectively stop ascribing worth to certain social dissimilarities. Would that not be a great help in coming to practice Kierkegaard's own advice—to hold dissimilarity loosely?

In a way, this is what Kierkegaard himself has done in his critique of striving for superiority. His argument is that it erases unique features of each person, diminishes our common humanity, and makes our lives revolve around harmful fictions. If we were to take the obligation to treat the poor, rather than our friends and the lofty, to banquets and apply it to the "blue eyes" problem, would not loving each person equally and no one exceptionally nudge us to reflect on how to change structures that grant exceptional status to some forms of beauty? More broadly, if we accept Kierkegaard's critique of striving for superiority, what would stand in the way of working against structures that encourage striving for superiority?

# 3

# Satan's Aspiration (Milton)

I n John Milton's *Paradise Lost* and *Paradise Regained*, striving
for superiority—striving to best a competitor—is at the heart
of the human condition. Human striving for superiority over
other humans, though, is set within the larger, cosmic striving
of the most exalted of all angelic beings, Satan, for preeminence
over the one God. Given the war in heaven unleashed by Satan's
striving, it is tempting to describe this as a contest for superiority
between Satan and God, with humans as unlucky casualties. But
that would be only half right—right only about Satan. Milton
distinguishes clearly between the Creator and creatures, both terrestrial and angelic. Even resisting Satan—better: *precisely in* resisting Satan—God remains untouched by striving for superiority.
In an important sense, God struggles not to prevent Satan from
taking God's throne, which would be, by definition, impossible.
God struggles, rather, to protect the creatures, made in the image
of the One who does not strive for superiority, from plunging each
other into the abyss in the very struggle to elevate themselves above
others. In *Paradise Regained*, the incarnate God wins victory over
Satan by *refusing* to pursue the project of becoming the greatest.

I know no author who explores the moral psychology of striving for superiority more insightfully than Milton in *Paradise Lost* and *Paradise Regained*. As I read these texts, Milton does not explain why Satan strives to be superior to God—or why Eve, after being successfully tempted by Satan, strives to be superior to Adam. In the scene in *Paradise Lost* that reaches furthest into the history of Satan's relation to God, we encounter him plagued by a sense of inferiority to God, simultaneously dejected and burning to be greater—which, in this case, means being absolutely the greatest. Milton explores in great detail how such striving shapes and degrades one's perception of oneself and one's social and natural environments. In doing so, he also illuminates possible ways to push against striving for superiority and opens a window to a life beyond the pain of inferiority and striving for superiority. What he does not do is give reason for Satan's rebellion. I will follow suit and leave the *why* unexplored.

===⊞===

Milton was a passionate egalitarian. In his early tract "The Tenure of Kings and Magistrates" (1648), he writes that no human who knows anything "can be so stupid to deny that all men naturally were born free, being the image and resemblance of God himself, and were by privilege above all the creatures, born to command and not to obey."[1] All humans are born equal and free, which is one important reason he pushes hard against striving for superiority. Yet he is not opposed to all hierarchy. As C. S. Lewis notes in *A Preface to Paradise Lost*, Milton in fact subscribed to a hierarchical conception of the universe:

> Everything except God has some natural superior; everything except unformed matter has some natural inferior. The goodness, happiness, and dignity of every being consists in obeying its natural superior and ruling its natural inferiors. When it fails in either part of this twofold task we have disease or monstrosity in the scheme of things until the peccant being is either destroyed or corrected.[2]

The hierarchical view of reality and the claim that *all* humans are "born to command" may not seem to fit his egalitarianism, but it does. Humans are to command not each other but those below them; they ought to rule, as Genesis puts it, "over the fish of the sea and over the birds of the air and over every living thing that moves upon the earth" (1:28).

In my own text, I have rendered Milton's "all men" as "all humans," which is correct, in one sense, from Milton's perspective: it marks humans, men and women, as distinct from and superior to animals. But there is also a sense in which Milton means "all men" to be read more narrowly—as all human males. Women, he believes, are inferior to men, even in paradise, and after the fall this inferiority became a relationship of subjection. As I will argue later, the tension between Eve's equality to Adam as a human and her alleged inferiority to him as a woman plays a key role in Milton's account of the fall. Milton is not against God ruling over all creatures; men, after the fall, ruling over women; and women and men ruling over animals. God is Adam's natural superior; Adam is Eve's natural superior; Adam and Eve together are animals' natural superiors. Milton was a limited egalitarian. He was against monarchs and bishops. They are humans ruling over other humans—or, rather, males ruling over other males.

Milton's concern with striving for superiority does not, then, have to do with the *fact* of superiority. That some are superior to others is simply the reality of the hierarchical ordering of life (and that some are superior to others *in some regard* is the reality of *any* ordering of life). Milton is against *striving* for superiority, against the ambition to usurp and hold the position of superiority—whether by one person over their natural equals or by an inferior person over their natural superiors. In *Paradise Lost* (*PL*), there is one important example of striving for superiority among equals: Nimrod, of Genesis 10, is the paradigmatic tyrannical ruler over equals who seeks a name for himself "regardless whether good or evil fame" (*PL* 12:47). Milton alludes to Nimrod only briefly in his great poem and leaves that seeker of a great and lasting name nameless.

The two key strivers for superiority in *Paradise Lost* are Satan and Eve. Satan, an angel and therefore a creature, is a natural inferior to God but strives illicitly for the position of superiority over God, his natural superior. Eve is both Adam's equal and Adam's inferior, and Milton describes her as striving ultimately not so much to gain equality with Adam but to invert the order of gendered superiority between them. From my perspective, Milton is simply wrong in ascribing superiority to men and inferiority to women—but his account of Eve's striving, rendered so plausibly, is nevertheless highly illuminating.

Such striving is characteristic of human relations not just in hierarchical societies but in all societies in which relatively stable differences play a role—differences in physical power, intellectual capacities, know-how, wealth, and more. As I showed in chapter 1, they are particularly pronounced in societies in which competition is a structurally defining feature of human relations. If this is true, then the tension between equality and difference, and the resulting striving for superiority that is central to Milton's account of the fall, is at work in most societies with which we are familiar.

Milton scholars note the aspiration to superiority in both Satan and Eve, especially in the case of Eve. They tend to treat it, however, as if it were marginal to their characters, a kind of excess in their search for liberation rather than its key motivator. In contrast, I will argue that it is central to both Satan's and Eve's characters and the key reason for their fall.

# 1

The first time Satan speaks in *Paradise Lost* is in a conversation with Beelzebub, his second in command. Along with their entire army, legions of angels, they are in hell, having been hurled from heaven for rebellion "against the throne and monarchy of God"

(*PL* 1:43). Satan has now recovered from the initial shock of defeat and is beginning to plan his next move. Early in the conversation, he explains why he went to war against God. It was, he says, from a "sense of injured merit" (*PL* 1:98). God held him down, denied him what was rightly his. For Lewis, the perceived unfairness in the way God treated Satan, the arbitrariness of it, is the main reason for Satan's rebellion.[3] As I see it, Satan's sense of "injured merit" is more the occasion and excuse for rebellion than the original and main reason for it.

To understand what injured Satan's sense of merit, we need to hear the explanation the archangel Raphael gives to Adam as to why he and Eve should be on guard against the fallen Satan. Raphael informs Adam of Satan's plan to entice Adam and Eve to disobedience, spoil God's new world, and integrate it into Satan's kingdom. In the process, he speaks about the reason for Satan's malevolence. Before the world was created, the Father appointed the Son to be the head of the entire angelic host, their Lord (*PL* 5:604–15). Every knee was to bow before him, acknowledging his lordship; obedience to him was obedience to the Father. The entire angelic host seemed pleased, singing and dancing for joy on God's sacred hill. God, too, was rejoicing, though not in the Son's superiority but in the joy of the angels (*PL* 5:641).

"All seemed" pleased, Raphael says. In their admiration they looked as if they were standing in a happy relation to superiority, as Kierkegaard puts it.[4] "But all were not" pleased, Raphael adds (*PL* 5:617). Satan, the "first Archangel, great in power, / in favor and pre-eminence" (*PL* 5:660–61), was, in fact, very displeased. Proud of his eminence, he "thought himself impaired" (*PL* 5:665). As the Lord of heavenly hosts, the Son was now Satan's Lord as well. By appointing the Son as the Lord, the Father had diminished Satan, making him inferior. The way Satan presents the event to his subordinates, this was a case of nepotism, the preferential treatment of a close relation, to Satan's detriment. This is the grave divine injustice that led Satan to wage war against the throne. In fact, however, Satan was distorting the nature of the relation of God both to Satan and to the Son. That distortion, too, and not just the rebellion that it sought to legitimize, was the poisoned fruit of Satan's "unhappy" relation to the reality of God's superiority over him.

=== iii ===

Whether the Father acted unjustly in elevating the Son turns on the respective places of the Son and Satan in the great chain of being. If the Son is a creature, then Satan has a case. Satan is then on the same plane of being as the Son, and given Satan's eminence, the Son's elevation is arbitrary. But if the Son is a co-Creator with the Father, then Satan has no case. Milton makes just this point as the archangel Abdiel tries to dissuade Satan and the angelic hosts from war. He argues that the Son is not a creature but the Word by which the Father made all things, "ev'n thee, and all the Spirits of Heav'n" (*PL* 5:837).[5] Together with the Father, the Son is the divine Creator; together with all angels, Satan is a creature. The Son, along with the Father, made Satan to be the first archangel, crowning both Satan and all angels with glory (*PL* 5:836–38). No merit of Satan's was injured.[6] He is rebelling not against injustice done to him but against his own ontological inferiority. He is fighting not for justice but for preeminence. He is a creature striving to be superior to the Creator.

To justify the grand insurrection and to motivate the angels gathered around him to take part in it, Satan has to contest Abdiel's claim that angels were created. Here we witness how striving for superiority often requires a justifying ideology that distorts reality.

> We know no time when we were not as now;
> Know none before us, self-begot, self-raised
> By our own quick'ning power, when fatal [inevitable] course
> Had circled his full orb, the birth mature
> Of this our native Heav'n, ethereal sons. (*PL* 5:859–64)

The claim is false, and Satan knows it. But he needs a lie to avoid losing troops if he is to win his war against God. There is a grain of truth to this lie: in the way God works, divine creation and earth's generation are not exclusive alternatives. For example, on the sixth day of creation, God made living things by commanding the earth to bring them forth (*PL* 7:453–56). Satan, however, takes the generative power of creation itself to exclude God's ultimate agency in creation. His conclusion is thus one-sided and false.[7] To legitimize itself publicly, striving for superiority creates its own truth: in this case, a false claim of self-generation as the foundation stone of angelic ontology.

—※—

In the conversation with Beelzebub and the exchange with Abdiel, Satan names the injustice of the Son's elevation as the reason for rebellion. Even as he complains about injured merit, however, we get an inkling that the elevation of the Son into the position of universal lordship has only exacerbated his preexisting grievance. After the Father declares that in heaven every knee shall bow to the Son, Satan not only tells the angels assembled around him that the knee-tribute is a "prostration vile" but also adds that the requirement of worship is "too much to one, but double how endured, / to one and to his image now proclaimed?" (*PL* 5:782–84). Worship of the Father alone is *already* "too much." Elevation of the Son is a problem for Satan, but bending the knee before God is what he disdains most.

Satan's famous soliloquy, undistorted by the rhetorical demands of an audience either of followers or opponents, reveals the key to his motivations most clearly—and it highlights viscerally the torment of inferiority and the seemingly irresistible desire for superiority. Before embarking on a clandestine operation in the garden of Eden, the defeated and exiled Satan remembers with agony "what he was, what he is, and what must be" (*PL* 4:25).[8] In telling the tale of his own fall, he elaborates on the reasons for rebellion against God. The soliloquy itself takes place after the elevation of the Son and Satan's subsequent war and defeat, but in it he remembers experiences in heaven that *preceded* the elevation of the Son. Addressing the brightly shining sun at its zenith, he says with a sigh,

> O thou that with surpassing glory crowned,
> Look'st from thy sole dominion like the God
> Of this new world; at whose sight all the stars
> Hide their diminished heads; to thee I call,
> But with no friendly voice, and add thy name
> O sun, to tell thee how I hate thy beams
> That bring to my remembrance from what state
> I fell, how glorious once above thy sphere;
> Till pride and worse ambition threw me down
> Warring in Heav'n against Heav'n's matchless King:
> Ah wherefore! he deserved no such return
> From me, whom he created what I was
> In that bright eminence, and with his good
> Upbraided none; nor was his service hard. (*PL* 4:32–45)

In a moment of pained honesty and regret—"Ah wherefore!"— Satan explains the reason for starting the civil war against his "matchless King." We hear nothing about injured merit. Just the opposite: the war was an evil return for good received. This admission suggests that he invented "injured merit" not just for political and military reasons but to ease the pain of self-loathing. The sense of injured merit allows him to ascribe his lower position to injustice suffered rather than to a lack on his part. Frustrated striving for superiority often seeks relief in the form of aggressive self-deception in which the superior is cast as morally deficient, arrogant, and oppressive, as Nietzsche argues in *On the Genealogy of Morality*.[9]

The war against God was outrageously unjust and, as Satan knew, utterly futile. So why proceed? Here is Satan's explanation, his explicitly stated motivation: "lifted up so high / I 'sdained subjection and thought one step higher / Would set me highest" (*PL* 4:49–50). Just because he was so eminent—the most eminent of all God's creatures, second only to the Creator—Satan could not abide having a superior over him: not just the Son but, above all, the Father. In terms of the likelihood of success, the desire to make that "one step higher" was nonsensical, but he could not resist making it, his desire clouding his judgment. An "unbounded hope" (*PL* 4:60) fueled his ambition,[10] and such ambition, he admits, is worse than pride (*PL* 4:40). He wanted to dethrone God and set himself in God's place, not to be equal but superior to God.[11] That's why, after he had failed to best God but succeeded in dividing God's empire, he still hopes that he might bring humanity to his side and so to reign over "more than half" (*PL* 4:111–12).[12]

Milton's Satan is not a freedom fighter pursuing justice, though he likes to portray himself as such. He is a rebel against his own creaturehood and inferiority to God. He admits this eloquently when he claims that "all [God's] good"—God's goodness as the Creator of just such a magnificent being as Satan was, God's goodness as the One who upbraided no one and whose service was easy—"prov'd ill in me, / And wrought but malice" (*PL* 4:48–49).

When we turn to Eve, we will see the desire for superiority over fellow creatures—also with destructive results. A creature's desire for superiority over another creature is problematic but, in a sense, understandable—it is achievable in theory, even if (in some cases) hard to attain. On the other hand, a creature's desire for superiority over the Creator is deranged. The word may seem too strong. But the distance in eminence of being between a creature and the Creator is "infinite" (see *PL* 4:408–11), and the creature owes to the Creator the continued existence of its own rebelling self. Satan acknowledges that comprehensive debt when he is alone with his thoughts: God created "what I was in that bright eminence" (*PL* 4:44). Satan's goal is not just insurmountably difficult but logically impossible. And yet, captive to striving for superiority, he pursues it.

## 2

Consider the effect of striving for superiority on how Satan experiences the gratitude that the gifts of existence and of eminence should elicit. Along with praise, gratitude was the *only* debt Satan owed his Creator.

> What could be less than to afford him praise,
> The easiest recompense, and pay him thanks,
> How due! Yet all his good proved ill in me,
> And wrought but malice; lifted up so high
> I 'sdained subjection, and thought one step higher
> Would set me highest, and in a moment quit
> The debt immense of endless gratitude,
> So burdensome, still paying, still to owe;
> Forgetful what from him I still received,
> And understood not that a grateful mind
> By owing owes not, but still pays, at once
> Indebted and discharged; what burden then? (*PL* 4:46–57)

Satan owes God thanks for who he is, but such gratitude is intolerable to him because inferiority to God is unbearable. To be grateful to God for the gift of existence is to recognize God's superiority. He must therefore deny this debt.

When Satan articulates what gratitude actually consists in, it turns out not to be burdensome at all. Gratitude is joyful recognition of the gift received, and that is all the payment necessary. Existence is a genuine gift, not a clandestine loan whose repayment in ceaseless gratitude and praise is intended to increase the reputational wealth of the divine benefactor. Satan knows that gratitude to God *discharges* the debt by simply acknowledging it,[13] that a grateful person is at once "indebted and discharged." But he does not want to know what he knows and still experiences gratitude as burdensome. What is burdensome, though, is not gratitude itself but what it implies: that he is not the highest, that he is not God.[14]

Like any creature, Satan owes more to God than gratitude, though grateful recognition of the gift received is all God requires. In failing to give thanks, Satan is injuring *God's merit*; he is refusing to give God even a fraction of what is due to God. Satan's complaint about his own injured merit is not just hollow but perverse. In a passage from *Paradise Regained* that echoes Satan's soliloquy, Christ makes just that point, as I will show shortly.

The unquenchable desire to be superior to God holds Satan captive. He cannot free himself from it. He finds himself unable to repent in order to be restored to his original position of preeminence among the angels because that would mean acknowledging his own inferiority to God. And even if he were to repent and obtain "by act of grace" his former state, the repentance would not last. How soon, he asks rhetorically, "would height recall high thoughts, how soon unsay / What feigned submission swore" (*PL* 4:95–96). Striving for superiority, not comfort or the absence of pain, is his highest value, his obsession. Moreover, repentance, if it were to occur, would bring him unbearable shame among his followers. He seduced them to believe, as he puts it, "that I could subdue / Th' Omnipotent" (*PL* 4:85–86).[15] Striving for superiority, Satan is unable to act in his own best interest. Faced with the choice either to be the highest or not to be at all, he will choose nothingness—or everlasting misery.

Fueling Satan's striving for superiority is his self-loathing at not being the highest—an extreme version of a poisonous sentiment that comes in many gradations.

> Ay me, they [his subordinates] little know
> How dearly I abide that boast so vain,

Under what torments inwardly I groan;
While they adore me on the throne of Hell,
With diadem and sceptre high advanced
The lower still I fall, only supreme
In misery; such joy ambition finds. (*PL* 4:86–92)

His aspiration to elevate himself above God and his boast to his followers that he can accomplish the feat define his whole being. But it is an impossible aspiration and an empty boast. Even as he is celebrated on the throne of hell, he is mired in self-loathing. That misery is the "joy" of a vain striving for superiority. "Me miserable! Which way shall I fly / Infinite wrath, and infinite despair? / Which way I fly is Hell; myself am Hell" (*PL* 4:73–75). The obverse of the affliction of inferiority, striving for superiority over God, *is* hell, whether one happens to be in heaven or hell. So where did Satan decide to fly?

All hope excluded thus, behold instead
Of us outcast, exiled, his new delight,
Mankind created, and for him this world.
So farewell hope, and with hope farewell fear,
Farewell remorse: all good to me is lost;
Evil be thou my good; by thee at least
Divided empire with Heav'n's King I hold
By thee, and more than half perhaps will reign;
As man ere long, and this new world shall know.
(*PL* 4:105–12)

Satan remains captive to the evil of striving for superiority and is therefore attached to all the other evils he needs to commit to continue the struggle. If he cannot conquer God and must dwell in hell, at least he can hope to ruin God's new world and make his own kingdom larger than God's. Supreme he will be, in at least one respect, any respect—by any means possible. Frustrated striving for superiority can turn to diminishing the competitor by destroying the very things in which the competitor delights.

**3**

Satan's striving for superiority is unbounded: "Better to reign in Hell" and seek to expand its domain than be second to God and "serve in Heav'n" (*PL* 1:260).[16] Eve's striving for superiority in *Paradise Lost* is more circumscribed. She is not tempted with the prospect of being greater than God or ruling a realm larger than God's. She is tempted into vying for superiority with her partner, Adam. As I will show, though, even for her, influenced as she is by Satan, the horizon for seeking superiority over Adam is the image of herself as the very best of creatures, angels included—in fact, it is the prospect of putting off humanity and putting on God (*PL* 9:713–14). (The formulation "putting off" the human and "putting on" God is an echo of Philippians 2, where Christ is said to have done the exact opposite: to have taken off the form of God and put on the form of a human servant. In their fall, Adam and Eve are anti-types of Christ; see chap. 4.) Striving for superiority does not end until one is the best—and even then, not if competitors are around.

In *Paradise Lost*, we first encounter Eve and Adam when Satan, disguised as a serpent, enters the garden. "Undelighted," he is observing "all delight" of paradise (*PL* 4:286), underscoring how striving for superiority distorts even the perception of good and joyful things. Satan sees new living creatures, and among them

> Two of far nobler shape erect and tall,
> Godlike erect, with native honour clad
> In naked majesty seemed lords of all,
> And worthy seemed, for in their looks divine
> The image of their glorious Maker shone,
> Truth, wisdom, sanctitude severe and pure,
> Severe, but in true filial freedom placed;
> Whence true authority in men; though both
> Not equal, as their sex not equal seemed;
> For contemplation he and valour formed,

For softness she and sweet attractive grace,
He for God only, she for God in him. (*PL* 4:288–99)

Satan identifies two features of Adam's and Eve's relation to each other. This is not merely Satan's perspective, for non-satanic observers share it as well. But the features are important for Satan because he will use them in his successful temptation.

First, Adam and Eve are *equal as humans*. They have some key attributes in common that distinguish them from and, in Milton's view, make them superior to all other earthlings. Both are erect and dignified, majestic lords of all. Each is an image of God and free— except for "one restraint," one "easy charge," binding for both of them equally: "of all the trees / In Paradise that bear delicious fruit / So various, not to taste that only Tree / Of Knowledge," as Adam puts it to Eve (*PL* 4:421–24; cf. 1:32).

Second, Adam and Eve are *differently gendered*.[17] As such, they are distinct not only in the way each looks but above all, in Milton's view, in the purpose for which each was created, and therefore also in their respective capacities. Adam was created for contemplation and valor, Eve for softness and attractive grace. This could suggest that bodily differences are simply that—differences rather than indicators of inequality. But immediately after reading of their respective qualities, we read what has become one of the most infamous lines in *Paradise Lost*: "He for God only, she for God in him." Milton's Eve is equal to Adam as a human but inferior to him as a woman in the all-defining relationship to God: Eve's relationship to God is mediated by Adam. Eve is also intellectually inferior to Adam—"in the mind / And inward faculties" (*PL* 8:541–42). Adam's superiority is visible, inscribed into the character of his body: Adam's "fair large front and eye sublime declared absolute rule," and Eve's "slender waist" suggests "subjection." Even the way they wear their hair symbolizes his rule and her subjection: "his parted forelock manly hung" and her hair fell down "as a vail" (*PL* 4:300–308). For Milton, these characteristics of each, though good, are arranged in a hierarchical order. He has taken the hierarchical relation between men and women and its symbolizations from the apostle Paul (1 Cor. 11:2–16). But Milton fails to note that in Paul's image of the church as the body of Christ, in whom there is "no longer male and female" (Gal. 3:28), each member is worthy of the same care and is to be accorded equal honor (see chap. 4).

=== ⊞ ===

Eve's *experience* of the difference between herself and Adam is central in the story of the temptation. In the very first scene after God creates her, Eve leans over a pool and sees, in its surface, a creature that looks at her "with sympathy and love" (*PL* 4:465). Eve takes an innocent delight in the beauty of the creature she does not yet know is herself—nothing like the awed attachment to self-image that we often associate with Narcissus, so engrossed that he is finally unable to move.[18] Satan's temptation, however, will exploit just that innocent self-delight. A voice, not Satan's, explains to her that she is seeing only a reflected image of herself and directs her to Adam, whose living image she is (*PL* 4:471). When she sees Adam, she immediately compares him with the image she now knows is herself. She finds him not just different from her but inferior: "less fair, / Less winning soft, less amiably mild, / Than that smooth wat'ry image"—and she turns back uninterested (*PL* 4:478–80).[19] This, too, is a comparative judgment of aesthetic worth and is still innocent, though insufficiently informed from Milton's perspective. Eve prefers the way she looks to the way Adam looks.

As she begins to walk away, Adam calls her back—"Return, fair Eve" (*PL* 4:481)—and informs her that God created her out of his side, that she is his "other half." Eve's perspective now shifts. Free as she is, she can either accept the implication of her originary dependence on Adam or not; she can either continue to walk away or return. Speaking to Adam, she explains her return: "with that thy gentle hand / Seized mine, I yielded and from that time see / How beauty is excelled by manly grace / And wisdom, which alone is truly fair" (*PL* 4:488–91). Importantly, her relationship as an inferior to a superior is marked by the tension between her attraction and her insight. It is held together only by Adam's gentleness and Eve's yielding. But Adam is not always exactly gentle, Satan is cunning, and the tension will prove difficult to sustain.

At one level, Eve freely accepts her inferiority. But the reader senses her discomfort with it. The best example of such unease is found in the so-called separation scene (*PL* 9:205–383). Adam resists her suggestion that they work in the garden separately and insists that she needs his protection from the Tempter, who is on a mission to destroy them. In the process, Adam both underscores Eve's inferiority and reasserts his own superiority.

> Leave not the faithful side
> That gave thee being, still shades thee and protects.
> The wife, where danger or dishonour lurks,
> Safest and seemliest by her husband stays,
> Who guards her, or with her the worst endures.
>     (*PL* 9:265–69)

Eve believes that Adam's argument against their working separately in the garden "inferiorizes" her. Apparently, she cannot be trusted to overcome the temptation on her own if she encounters the cunning Tempter, because her faith is not sincere enough and she is not wise enough to withstand it (cf. *PL* 9:320). She is annoyed at what she thinks is an unreasonable suggestion that they are "not endued / Single with like defense, whatever met" (*PL* 9:324–25). She responds,

> And what is faith, love, virtue unassayed
> Alone, without exterior help sustained?
> Let us not then suspect our happy state
> Left so imperfect by the Maker wise,

As not secure to single or combined.
Frail is our happiness, if this be so,
And Eden were no Eden thus exposed. *(PL 9:335–41)*

Eve argues that she cannot have Adam hover protectively over her, treating her as if she were a child; she must be free and trusted to be capable of withstanding the foe on her own. Untried, her virtue is no virtue; if she is too feeble to withstand trial, then Eden is not Eden for her. She, too, was created in God's image, not just in Adam's. Adam may be superior to her in intellect, but it is Satan's position, and should not be Adam's, that by herself woman is "opportune to all attempts" *(PL 9:481)*.

Eve, deemed intellectually inferior, wins the argument with Adam—and Adam yields. In fact, we suspect that Milton agrees with Eve's reasoning, given the similarities it bears to the key argument in *Areopagitica* (1644), his masterful defense of religious freedom.[20]

## 4

Eve is smart enough and virtuous enough to be capable of withstanding the temptation. And yet she will fall. Satan will exploit her ambivalence toward Adam's superiority, an ambivalence that rests on Milton's construal of her tension-laden positionality as both Adam's equal and his inferior.

After flattering Eve as "sov'reign mistress" and "sole wonder" and telling her that she is the object of his "gaze insatiate," Satan continues,

> Fairest resemblance of thy Maker fair,
> Thee all things living gaze on, all things thine
> By gift, and thy celestial beauty adore
> With ravishment beheld, there best beheld
> Where universally admired; but here
> In this enclosure wild, these beasts among,

Beholders rude, and shallow to discern
Half what in thee is fair, one man except,
Who sees thee? (and what is one?) who shouldst be seen
A goddess among gods, adored and served
By angels numberless, thy daily train. (*PL* 9:532–48)

Building on Eve's initial preference for her own looks over Adam's, Satan suggests that her superior beauty hasn't found proper recognition. Only beasts, who can't sufficiently appreciate beauty, and one other human see her. She deserves the adoration and service of the entire heavenly host. She deserves the position Satan himself thought ought to have been his. Eve knows that Satan is flattering her—she notes to him "thy overprizing" (*PL* 9:615)—but she also believes him, once more a case of knowing and not knowing. Those who strive for superiority will often lie and flatter if that is what it takes to achieve superiority; those who experience themselves as inferior will find themselves believing flattering lies as they seek relief. Eve's striving for superiority starts with Satan helping her imagine herself as superior.

Next, Satan takes up the critical issue of Eve's intellectual capacities, which are at the core of her inferior status. Adam and Satan—when the latter is not dissimulating—seem to agree that she is Adam's intellectual inferior.[21] Though Milton's Eve appears to agree with their assessment, she is uncomfortable with the idea. Her discomfort is Satan's opportunity, structurally built into the nature of the hierarchical relations between Adam and Eve. For the hierarchical system to work, it is not enough for the superiors to function as they ought (as Adam, in Milton's view, does). The inferiors also need to accept themselves as inferiors and consent to being in their place—in Eve's case, under Adam's guidance as her intellectual superior. When this happens, the inferiors can be properly integrated into a functioning whole. But Milton's Eve never fully accepts her inferiority.

Listening to Satan's eloquence, she wonders how a mere beast, as she takes the disguised Satan to be, has acquired the capacity to reason and speak. The miracle happened, he responds, when he ate the fruit of a certain "goodly tree," the tree of the knowledge of good and evil (*PL* 9:576). Changes began, and

> Thenceforth to speculations high or deep
> I turned my thoughts, and with capacious mind
> Considered all things visible in heav'n,
> Or earth, or middle, all things fair and good;
> But all that fair and good in thy divine
> Semblance, and in thy beauty's Heav'nly ray
> United I beheld; no fair to thine
> Equivalent or second, which compelled
> Me thus, though importune perhaps, to come
> And gaze, and worship thee of right declared
> Sov'reign of creatures, universal dame. (*PL* 9:602–12)

The fruit of the tree increased Satan's intellectual capacities. Endowed with the wisdom of the tree, he can understand Eve's value and potential better than she understands it herself. He sees all the good in the entire universe united in her. If Eve tastes of the fruit, he intimates, she will have no equal among all the creatures, earthly and heavenly, not just in beauty but in intellect as well.

Like the serpent, Eve will also come to understand what God must have meant in issuing the command not to eat from the tree. Even before eating its fruit, with the help of the talking serpent, Eve has come to know that there is no gain in not knowing the good and therefore no gain from not eating from the tree of the knowledge of good—and evil. She argues that the "good unknown, sure is not had, or had / and yet unknown, is not had at all" (*PL* 9:756–57). But that could not be God's intention; God would not intentionally keep humans "low and ignorant" (*PL* 9:704).

Once Eve eats her fill of the forbidden fruit, the first benefit she hopes to acquire is to "grow in maturity / In knowledge, as the gods who know all things" (*PL* 9:803–4). Among creatures, her knowledge will be supreme. She will no longer be Adam's intellectual

71

inferior but in two most important regards his superior. She has a solution to what she now sees clearly as a pressing problem but before her conversation with Satan had sensed as a mere discomfort.[22]

=== ‖ ===

Eve eats and feels liberated from her inferiority to Adam. But liberated to what? To a new partnership with Adam as equals—or to a new standing in a relationship assumed to be inevitably rivalrous?[23] The answer comes as she deliberates whether to tell Adam that she has disobeyed God's command.

> But to Adam in what sort
> Shall I appear? shall I to him make known
> As yet my change, and give him to partake
> Full happiness with me, or rather not,
> But keep the odds of knowledge in my power
> Without copartner? so to add what wants
> In female sex, the more to draw his love,
> And render me more equal, and perhaps,
> A thing not undesirable, sometime
> Superior; for inferior who is free? (PL 9:816–25)

Eve has been Adam's inferior her entire life. She now discounts her previous freedom to yield to Adam and deems all inferiority as a state not of limited freedom but of bondage. To be superior is to be truly free, she now thinks[24]—and to be attractive as well, to "draw [the] love" of others to oneself. But as she herself experiences, more often than not, striving for superiority inferiorizes others and invites rivalry and aggression, hence her exquisite ambivalence: keeping the fruit away from Adam will render her not just "more equal" but, "perhaps, a thing not undesirable, sometime superior."[25]

In the end, Eve decides to tell Adam. The reason, however, is not her moral commitment to equality but insecurity about her new superior standing and a fear of falling into even greater inferiority.

> But what if God have seen,
> And death ensue? then I shall be no more,
> And Adam wedded to another Eve,
> Shall live with her enjoying, I extinct;
> A death to think. Confirmed then I resolve,
> Adam shall share with me in bliss or woe:
> So dear I love him, that with him all deaths
> I could endure, without him live no life. (*PL* 9:826–33)

The deliberation ends with a declaration of love: "So dear I love him." But her love for Adam is dripping with self-regard, and even this compromised love does not seem the main reason why she decides to share the poisonous fruit with Adam. Considering the possibility that God may have seen and will punish her for the transgression with extinction, she will settle for equality, even if it turns out to be equality in death, rather than have Adam continue alive, enjoying another Eve—and being, in the end, even more superior. She will risk killing Adam in order not to return to a state of inferiority.[26]


## 5

Writing about the immediate aftermath of the fall, Milton describes the relational turmoil that ensues as both Adam and Eve continue vying for superiority amid their guilt. After a night of passionate but unhappy lovemaking (why does Milton mention passionate lovemaking after the fall?), as the weight of the consequences of knowing both good and evil, "good lost, and evil got" (*PL* 9:1072), is dawning on them, Adam begins what, predictably, turns into bitter mutual recrimination. Addressing Eve, he says,

> Would thou hadst hearkened to my words, and stayed
> With me, as I besought thee, when that strange
> Desire of wand'ring this unhappy morn,
> I know not whence possessed thee; we had then

Remained still happy, not as now, despoiled
Of all our good, shamed, naked, miserable. (*PL* 9:1134–39)

No, responds Eve, refusing to be blamed alone for their current state. In fact, you, Adam, "didst permit, approve, and fair dismiss" (*PL* 9:1159) what you now describe as my "wand'ring." It might have been Eve's idea to leave Adam's side, but after joint deliberation, he had come to think that she was right. "Was I to have never parted from thy side?" she asks him rhetorically. "As good have grown there still a lifeless rib" (*PL* 9:1154–55).

Adam is incensed and tells her that she despises his love, that she is ungrateful that he chose death to be with her rather than refuse the fruit and live. Milton concludes book 9 noting, "Thus they in mutual accusation spent / The fruitless hours, but neither self-condemning, / And of their vain contest appeared no end" (*PL* 9:1187–89). Here we see some of the negative underbelly of striving for superiority: each pushing the other down, insisting the other is worse.

The end of pushing the other down in seeking to climb up comes when Eve breaks the cycle of recrimination and acknowledges the part she played in their fall. We "both have sinned," Eve says to Adam, "but thou

Against God only, I against God and thee,
And to the place of judgement will return,
There with my cries importune Heaven, that all
The sentence from thy head removed may light
On me, sole cause to thee of all this woe,
Me me only just object of his ire. (*PL* 10:931–36)

Eve expresses a willingness to take the blame and punishment away from Adam. She is no longer pushing him down but lifting him up. She does this not as a way of acquiescing to inferiority but for the sake of the mutual peace that has been lost by their rivalrous jostling for position (*PL* 10:924–31). Adam's heart is softened toward her, and though he still lectures her, he expresses a similar sentiment:

> If prayers
> Could alter high decrees, I to that place
> Would speed before thee, and be louder heard,
> That on my head all might be visited,
> Thy frailty and infirmer sex forgiv'n,
> To me committed and by me exposed. (*PL* 10:953–58)

He is still eager to affirm his superiority but at the same time expresses willingness to take all the blame on himself and, in this one domain, to lower himself to elevate her.

This is the end of their fending off inferiority and jostling for superiority with respect to the colossal failure of eating the forbidden fruit. Adam concludes the "vain contest" by joining in Eve's confession of sin and her exhortation to peace between them and enmity toward Satan. He puts it in terms of the virtue most opposed to the vice of their foe.

> But rise, let us no more contend, nor blame
> Each other, blamed enough elsewhere, but strive
> In offices of love, how we may light'n
> Each other's burden in our share of woe. (*PL* 10:959–62)

Striving in love, seeking to bear each other's burdens, is the opposite of striving for superiority. It is striving for excellence. In Kierkegaard's terms, this would be striving to act like the prototype, Christ (see chap. 2).

## 6

In the two cases of striving for superiority I have examined in this chapter, they seem to be one-on-one affairs: Satan, the inferior, aspires to be superior to God; Eve, equal but inferior, aspires to be superior to Adam. But that isn't entirely right. First, in both cases there is a third party, observers before whose eyes the recognition of the aspired superiority takes place. In Satan's case, it is the entirety of the angelic host. His aspiration is not just to be superior to God but for the angels to recognize him as such—which would, of course, also increase his superiority to them. In Eve's case, Satan plants in her the dream of her superior beauty and intelligence being seen and recognized not only by Adam but also by all creatures, terrestrial and heavenly. The size of the audience increases the value of superiority and therefore the stakes of striving for it. A dominant feature of striving for superiority is that it seeks the admiring eyes of others; according to Rousseau (as I have shown in chap. 1), that is its chief motivation.

There is also another sense in which striving for superiority is not merely a matter of competition between two parties. Eve's striving for superiority over Adam and before all the angels was not a discrete event happening between them in front of the spectators. It was folded into Satan's striving for superiority; he was striving to win a contest with God by seeking to craft Eve—and, in his mind, through her all humanity—into his own self-loathing and ungrateful image. A striver for superiority herself, she was an unwitting tool in Satan's striving for superiority. Eve herself later made her son Cain a tool in her own striving and, in a sense, replicated in Cain's striving for superiority over Abel her own need for self-elevation. Strivers for superiority both are used as tools and use others as tools. When striving for superiority is a dominant value, everything potentially becomes fuel for the general bonfire of ambition.

But perhaps the converse can also be true. If humans can become tools caught in the diabolical web of striving for superiority, then they can also be caught up in Christ's contrary movement of love that seeks to serve and elevate others. Milton makes this point in *Paradise Regained*.

**7**

What is Milton's alternative to striving for superiority? Giving others their due? Though there is no explicit commandment in *Paradise Lost* stating "Thou shalt not injure anyone's merit!" both Satan and Eve indirectly affirm the principle by using it as private and public justification for their rebellions. But striving for superiority is compatible with giving others their due if greater merit is the value that motivates the striving. That's what a meritocracy is supposed to be all about: those with greater merit rule; they are rightly on the top, celebrated, legitimately superior. And yet in *Paradise Lost*, merit is not the foundation of social order. Satan did not work his way up to the greatest eminence among angels by competing fairly and winning; whatever his contribution was to his station, *God created* him to be eminent (*PL* 4:43–44). Paul, and Kierkegaard after him, pushes hard against merit as the basis for social standing (see chaps. 4 and 2, respectively).

Does this mean that striving for superiority is a problem mainly because one is supposed to stay gratefully in the place to which one was ordained by the Almighty? Perhaps the first commandment in heaven and on earth is "Thou shalt not rebel against God!" Is, then, the reason one should not strive for superiority God's insistence on God being the superior of all?

In *Paradise Regained*, the sequel to *Paradise Lost*, making superiority the chief good stands at odds with the whole Christian moral order. God is not the chief guardian of the order in which striving for superiority reigns supreme—the "great Forbidder," as Eve calls God at the time of her fall (*PL* 9:815). God is the *supreme exemplar* of the alternative, Christian moral order. In *Paradise Lost*, the contest between the Son and Satan concerns allegiance to God, and it is carried out by means of a battle. In *Paradise Regained* (PR), which tells "of deeds / Above heroic, though in secret done" (*PR* 1:15), allegiance to God is allegiance not mainly to the supreme power but to a moral vision of life that is fundamentally opposed to striving for superiority. The entire book is about the temptation of Christ in the wilderness, about Christ's undoing of what Eve and Adam had done. The Son is striving to overcome Satan, the great and original striver for superiority, who came to rule the earth by enticing the first human pair to strive for superiority. But in the way the Son overcomes temptation, he displays a moral vision that shows striving for superiority to be a poisonous and self-destructive vice and not merely the transgression of a limit set by an outside force, whether justly or arbitrarily.

━━━✠━━━

*Paradise Lost* ends with Eden destroyed and Satan in charge of the earth. Obsessed with striving to be the highest, Satan has succeeded in spoiling God's new world and increasing his own realm. Yet Satan fears for his rule; creaturely superiority is never secured, always tenuous. Even before Adam and Eve leave paradise, in cursing the serpent, God warns Satan that the one born of Eve's progeny, humanity's "great Deliverer," will bruise his head (*PL* 10:180–81, 12:148). In *Paradise Regained*, we first encounter Satan at Jesus's baptism. He hears the Father declare Jesus to be the "beloved Son" and is "nigh thunderstruck" (*PR* 1:35–36). This recalls the Son's prior victory over Satan when he sent "ten thousand thunders" and drove Satan with his armies "thunderstruck" into "the bottomless pit" (*PL* 6:834–66).

The puzzle is that the one declared to be the beloved Son looks just like any other human being. Satan undertakes to temp Jesus in the wilderness, largely to find out what *kind* of son of God he is—a son of God like any human being is, like all the angels are, including Satan, or, as Satan fears, *the* Son of God, the One seated at God's right hand (*PR* 4:514–25). Either way, Satan's goal is for Jesus to recognize Satan as his god—and therefore as his superior. This would be a double victory. At one level, Jesus is human and the representative of humanity; thus, if Satan wins a victory over him, as he won over Adam and Eve, he can keep him and all of humanity as his subjects. But if Jesus is the divine Son, then in succeeding Satan will have made the Son recognize Satan as God— which will mean winning the fight for superiority over God, a goal Satan has been striving for since the beginning.

Satan fails in both endeavors. At the end of the last temptation, at Jesus's declaration "Also it is written, / Tempt not the Lord thy God," Satan, "smitten with amazement," falls from the pinnacle of the temple (*PR* 4:562). Jesus discloses himself as unassailably divine, and Satan loses. Jesus wins this second victory not by wielding military-style power but by acting according to a value more basic and more divine than overpowering might.

# 8

The temptation to glory is central to the contest between the Son and Satan in the wilderness. At stake is not only the relative status of the Son and Satan but also the most basic values in God's universe, the condition for the genuine flourishing of God's creatures. Possessing the highest glory was Satan's chief motivation in heaven, and it remained his chief motivation when God gave him freedom to roam the earth. After Jesus successfully resists his temptation, Satan loses because he is "insatiable for glory" (*PR* 3:147–48). But Satan rightly sees glory as God's attribute as well; in the face of Christ, "glimpses of his Father's glory shine" (*PR* 1:86–93). The question, then, is not whether glory is good but what is truly glorious.

The temptations center on the question of glory: Satan tempts Jesus by comparing him with other humans who have striven to be the best, for he sees him as a person "made and set wholly on the accomplishment / Of greatest things" (*PR* 2:206–8). Since Satan associates being great with superiority, he tells Jesus that he cannot be great, let alone the greatest, in obscurity. Superiority demands recognition.

Affecting private life, or more obscure
In savage wilderness, wherefore deprive
All earth her wonder at thy acts, thyself
The fame and glory—glory, the reward
That sole excites to high attempts the flame
Of most erected spirits, most tempered pure
Aethereal, who all pleasures else despise,
All treasures and all gain esteem as dross,
And dignities and powers, all but the highest? (*PR* 3:22–30).

Satan's notable examples, with whom he invites Jesus to compare himself, are Alexander the Great, who by the age of thirty had created the largest empire in the ancient world, and Julius Caesar, "whom now all the world admires" and who "the more he grew in years, the more inflamed / With glory, wept that he had lived so long / Inglorious" (*PR* 3:39–42). This is the same Julius Caesar who, when he was young and passing through a small Alpine village, is reported to have said, "I would rather be first here than the second in Rome."[27] Satan implies that Jesus, thirty at the time of temptation, is lagging in achievement behind the great conquerors and claims that he can help Jesus rise to the highest glory. Jesus will be the greatest in the world if he worships Satan—thereby recognizing Satan's superiority over him. If Jesus were a human being out to achieve glory by ruling the world, it might seem like a good deal. Each would get what they want—except that, when superiority is the highest value, those who give feigned benevolence and can at any moment take away what has been given.

Jesus is unimpressed and, in his response, defines how glory ought to be properly understood. Human glory is "but a blaze of fame, / The people's praise," he says to Satan (*PR* 3:47–48). Most people don't know true glory; of them "to be dispraised were no small praise" (*PR* 3:51–56)! As to the great conquerors, those who count them glorious are gravely mistaken. True glory is attained without "ambition, war, or violence, by deeds of peace, by wisdom eminent"

(*PR* 3:90–91). For Milton's Jesus, the examples of true glory are Job and Socrates, not Alexander the Great and Julius Caesar.

Jesus ends his response by saying—as did Jesus in John's Gospel (8:50)—that he seeks not his own glory but the glory of the God who sent him. One should not seek one's own glory, Jesus implies, whether it comes from those who know what is truly glorious or not; one should seek God's glory and accept only the glory that comes from God's praise.

> This is true glory and renown—when God
> Looking on the Earth, with approbation marks
> The just man, and divulges him through Heaven
> To all his Angels, who with true applause
> Recount his praises. Thus he did to Job. . . .
> Famous he was in Heaven; on Earth less known,
> Where glory is false glory, attributed
> To things not glorious, men not worthy of fame.
>     (*PR* 3:60–64, 68–70)

Jesus seeks God's approbation, and he does so not by seeking his own glory but by advancing God's glory. He is after excellence, not superiority.

=== ··· ===

With Jesus committing himself to God's glory, Satan thinks that he now has an opening. Isn't God, whose Son Jesus claims to be, the greatest glory seeker of all?

> Think not so slight of glory, therein least
> Resembling thy great Father. He seeks glory,
> And for his glory all things made, all things
> Orders and governs; nor content in Heaven,
> By all his Angels glorified, requires
> Glory from men, from all men, good or bad,
> Wise or unwise, no difference, no exemption.

81

> Above all sacrifice, or hallowed gift,
> Glory he requires, and glory he receives,
> Promiscuous from all nations, Jew, or Greek,
> Or Barbarous, nor exception hath declared;
> From us, his foes pronounced, glory he exacts. (PR 3:109–20)

Glory is God's chief value, Satan claims. It is the chief end of all God's doings, and God insists on receiving it indiscriminately from everyone—from the discerning and the ignorant, from those who are good and those who are evil, from friends and from implacable foes. God's character and actions, Satan claims, contest Jesus's disparagement of glory. Glory is the highest good because it is God's highest good. God strives not just to *be* absolutely superior but to be *recognized and celebrated as* absolutely superior. Can that be wrong? Can God be wrong?

Jesus debunks Satan's argument with a response that echoes Satan's soliloquy in *Paradise Lost* about his self-loathing and incapacity for gratitude (PL 4:32–113). Explaining why and how God seeks to be glorified by everyone, Jesus says,

> Since his Word all things produced,
> Though chiefly not for glory as prime end,
> But to shew forth his goodness, and impart
> His good communicable to every soul
> Freely; of whom what could He less expect
> Than glory and benediction—that is, thanks—
> The slightest, easiest, readiest recompense
> From them who could return him nothing else,
> And, not returning that, would likeliest render
> Contempt instead, dishonour, obloquy?
> Hard recompense, unsuitable return
> For so much good, so much beneficence! (PR 3:122–33)

It is appropriate for God, and for God alone, to seek all glory, Jesus says to Satan—but only because God does not seek glory the way creatures do. God created all things and gives to all things their existence and their powers. The argument is not that because God created humans, God has both the authority and the power to demand that creatures glorify God. The argument is rather that human beings owe something to God for the gift of existence, and God is therefore the appropriate recipient of glory.

But what exactly is the glory God seeks? First, and by definition, it cannot be something that God needs. Satan is wrong that God's "prime end" in creating, preserving, and governing all things is God's own glory. If it were, then God would be seeking the enhancement of God's own good in everything God does. But God's good cannot be enhanced. The good that God is concerned with is the *good of creatures*. God's chief goal is "to shew forth his goodness" and to do so by imparting "his good communicable to every soul." The claim corresponds to what Milton says of God's glory in *Paradise Lost*: of all things that make up God's glory, "love without end, and without measure grace" shines the brightest (*PL* 3:142). Milton makes the comment in the context of redemption, but creation no less than redemption is an expression of God's generosity. God creates and gives freely and *does not need* anything in return. As I will show, Paul makes the same point—and makes it an argument against boasting, against feeling and claiming to be superior to another (chap. 4).

Second, the relation between God and creatures is such that creatures don't have anything of their own to give back to God, a point I will also explore in chapter 4. The existence and power of creatures over the entire span of their lives are God's gifts to them. Giving God a sacrifice or a sacred gift is giving to God out of what is already God's own. The only return gift that God requires is "glory and benediction," which mean, Milton adds, nothing more than "thanks." Gratitude isn't just "the easiest recompense," as Satan himself stated in *Paradise Lost* (4:47) and as Jesus underscores here. It is also the only recompense possible and the only one God asks.

Third, gratitude does not elevate God to the position of "the Highest"; it neither generates nor maintains nor magnifies God's superiority. Gratitude only recognizes with delight the good received from God. Similarly, a lack of gratitude in no way diminishes God. Ingrates, however, do fail to give God what is due. They also tend to harbor contempt for God that is born out of contempt for themselves as dependent creatures. In the case of Satan, all that God benevolently bestowed freely on him proved, as he reports in *Paradise Lost*, "ill in me, / And wrought but malice" (*PL* 4:48–49).

Since God is the source of all creatures' good, it is inappropriate for creatures to seek their own glory (though, as I will show, in Milton's view it is not inappropriate for them to receive and have glory!).

> But why should man seek glory, who of his own
> Hath nothing, and to whom nothing belongs
> But condemnation, ignominy, and shame—
> Who, for so many benefits received,
> Turned recreant to God, ingrate and false,
> And so of all true good himself despoiled;
> Yet, sacrilegious, to himself would take
> That which to God alone of right belongs? (*PR* 3:134–41)

The lines at the center of the quote contain a dismal view of every fallen human being: recreant, ingrate, false, of all true good despoiled, and worthy of condemnation, ignominy, and shame. They are implausibly negative words to come from the mouth of the Jesus we encounter in the Gospels. Yet the point that Milton's Jesus makes stands even if we agree only with the more basic claim about the nature of creaturehood: creatures, just because they are creatures, have nothing to claim as their own. As I will show and explore, Paul makes the same point in 1 Corinthians 4:7: "For who makes you different from another [and better]? What do you have that you did not receive? And if you received it, why do you boast as if you did not receive?" Those to whom everything is given should not boast. Ascribing glory to themselves for what they have received, they fail to recognize their own qualities as God's gifts. Gratitude directs attention back toward the giver of all good gifts; glory thus belongs to God. To seek it for oneself is to wrong God and arrogate to oneself what belongs to God.

Such a view of glory, Milton suggests, immunizes Jesus against succumbing to Satan's temptation. However, it might seem to come close to validating Satan's description of God. God is soaking up all the glory throughout creation so as to declare himself boastfully the highest; creatures are merely props for God's absolute superiority. But to say that glory belongs "of right" only to God as the Creator of everything is *not* to claim that God alone ends up with all the glory.

> Yet so much bounty is in God, such grace,
> That who advances his glory, not their own,
> Them he himself to glory will advance. *(PR* 3:142–44)

Satan's core argument is that if Jesus desires to be like his Father, then he should seek his own glory because his Father craves glory, insisting on getting it from anyone and everyone. Jesus responds that not only does God not seek glory in the way creatures do but also those who give glory to God receive glory from God—the only glory truly worth having.[28] Jesus says to Satan,

> This is true glory and renown—when God,
> Looking on the Earth, with approbation marks
> The just man, and divulges him through Heaven
> To all his Angels, who with true applause
> Recount his praises. Thus he did to Job,
> When, to extend his fame through Heaven and Earth,
> As thou to thy reproach may'st well remember,
> He asked thee, "Hast thou seen my servant Job?"
> Famous he was in Heaven; on Earth less known,

85

Where glory is false glory, attributed
To things not glorious, men not worthy of fame.
  (*PR* 3:60–70)

What matters is not fame or renown—to live in the tongues and
be in the talk of people (cf. *PR* 3:55). What matters is not one's
relative standing, one's perceived inferiority or superiority to others: how large one's empire is, how much wealth one has, how
influential one's intellectual contribution is in comparison with
that of others. What matters is whether one lives a life of goodness,
whether one is just (like Job) or truthful (like Socrates) (see *PR*
3:88–99). The only approbation worth taking seriously is that from
God, and the only applause that from the unfallen angels. This
glory belongs to those who embody and reflect God's goodness.

The effect of Jesus's reply to Satan is to redefine what is truly
glorious. Genuine goodness *is* glory. In gratitude, human beings
give glory to God for God's bountiful and free generosity; in marking a just man with approbation, God gives glory to generous, just,
and truthful human beings. Is there superiority and inferiority in
goodness among humans? If there is, those who are superior are
not praised for being *better than* those who are inferior. They are
praised for the excellence of their goodness—and none of them
boasts of this goodness, praising themselves for being its possessor.
Milton here echoes Paul.

———※———

My argument in this chapter has been that at the center of Milton's two great poems is a powerful critique of striving for superiority. In *Paradise Lost*, striving for superiority is Satan's chief
motivation for rebellion. This striving cloaks itself with the alleged
experience of injured merit; it spins a false story of self-creation
so as to make itself morally plausible. Satan's attempts to deceive
others culminate in his own self-deception, the deranged belief
that maybe he can somehow shake God's throne. Persisting in his

striving and clinging to self-deception, he loses his ability to take joy in his own original goodness and in the goodness of the world and robs himself of the possibility of redemption.

In her own way, Eve falls because she craved superiority as well—though to her credit, to make this pernicious ambition her own, she had to be tempted by someone else, whereas Satan was, as Milton puts it, "self-tempted" (*PL* 3:130). In both cases, a created order of inferiority and superiority is a factor as well; in Eve's case, the mix of hierarchy with a rightful claim to equality proves to be a volatile combination. A striving that at first seemed circumscribed grew boundless under the Tempter's influence. Restless comparisons, to use Kierkegaard's phrase, and ambition for superiority by both Adam and Eve end up poisoning what could have been a happy relationship—even as Adam and Eve try to reconcile, they try to outdo each other. Even love can be burdened and warped by the drive for superiority.

I have also argued that, from the perspective of *Paradise Regained*, these figures are anti-types of Jesus Christ. In his temptation by Satan—to seek wealth, rule, or wisdom and, in each of these, to aspire to the greatest glory—Christ refuses Satan's offer of help to become superior and to present himself as superior to all worldly competitors because that goal itself was wrong. At the end of his last temptation, Jesus is left standing alone on the pinnacle of the temple, where Satan had brought him. "Smitten with amazement" (*PR* 4:562) by Jesus's response to his last temptation, Satan falls, tumbling down not so much from the temple as from the height he had reached by successfully tempting Eve and Adam—just as he had previously tumbled into "the bottomless pit" after his insurrection in heaven (*PL* 6:834–66). Jesus stands on the pinnacle of the holiest of earthly places because of his refusal to strive for superiority. He enacts a vision of a moral universe where the highest good is God's free generosity, which needs nothing in return, and creatures' free gratitude, joyfully receiving their being from God and living it out in the world—in short, the call and response to love in freedom.

**9**

William Blake famously said that Milton himself was of Satan's party.[29] He was referring to a strong affinity one senses in the writer of *Paradise Lost* with the poem's main protagonist. While Milton does not finally side with the devil, perhaps Satan's portrayal is at times so sympathetic precisely because Milton himself felt acutely the temptation to strive for superiority. That the creator of two powerful poems, at the center of both of which is a critique of striving for superiority, might not have been able to triumph over the temptation is testimony to the power of this pervasively human and yet deeply misguided striving.

Young Milton had a burning ambition to exceptional greatness. Mark Pattison, Milton's nineteenth-century biographer, mentions a letter Milton sent in 1632 to a friend in Cambridge in which he wrote that his "mind was made and set wholly on the accomplishment of greatest things."[30] In *Paradise Regained*, Milton uses those same words to describe the attitude of Jesus (*PR* 2:207–8). But while it may be ambitious to liken his mission to that of Christ, perhaps this was no more than an aspiration to imitate Christ and a striving for creative excellence, a much different striving than striving for superiority (see chap. 1).

Still, Milton's early and extreme competitiveness can reasonably be described as striving for superiority. One of Milton's first English poems—written at age twenty-one and placed at the head of his first published collection of poetry sixteen years later—is titled "On the Morning of Christ's Nativity."[31] In the poem's prelude, he notes that it is "a present to the Infant God . . . to welcome him to his new abode" (16, 18). But the poem is not just about the arrival of the "heaven-descended King" and the King's purpose in coming. As John Rogers has argued, it is also about Milton's own beginning as a poet and the purpose of his poetic calling.[32]

In the last stanza of the prelude, Milton's own striving for superiority comes into full view.

> See how from far upon the Eastern road
> The Star-led Wizards haste with odors sweet:
> O run, prevent them with thy humble ode,
> And lay it lowly at his blessed feet;
> Have thou the honor first, thy Lord to greet,
> And join thy voice unto the Angel Choir,
> From out his secret Altar toucht with hallow'd fire. (22–28)

The last line suggests that Milton considers poetry his divine calling. It invokes the best-known calling in the Hebrew Bible, that of the prophet Isaiah. Like Isaiah's, Milton's lips are unclean; and like Isaiah, Milton wants them cleansed, touched with hallowed fire—with "a live coal" that the Seraph had "taken from the altar with a pair of tongs" (Isa. 6:6).

Divine calling and the need for purgation are not surprising, nor is it surprising that Milton would want to lay his "humble" ode "lowly" at Jesus's blessed feet. He is honoring the great God who was able and willing to assume a state in which the peals of the heavenly Voice's thunder had become "infant cries of our God."[33] And yet just as he is describing his poetic act as humbly giving a humble gift to a humble God, out of nowhere comes a powerful statement of his aspiration to superiority. Milton exhorts himself to run and arrive where the infant is before the Magi do so that he himself can have *the honor of being the first* to greet his Lord. What should it matter who comes first to honor the God who is willing to lay "stabling under a mean roof" even though he governs with his Father the realms above?[34] Why is Milton competing with pagan wise men from the East and not just "hasting" as they are? Why does he want to *outdo* them in honoring Christ? Might Milton not be dishonoring the humble God by being so concerned to arrive before others? Do we not see here a side of Milton that is, even in worship, a bit of Satan's party?[35]

There is yet another competition in the poem. Among the effects of Jesus's nativity, Milton discusses the downfall of the pagan gods, who "were suddenly destroyed in their own shrines," as he put it in a letter to his friend Charles Diodati.[36] "Our Babe," writes Milton in the nativity ode, "to show his Godhead true, / Can in his swaddling bands control the damned crew" (227–28). Milton's poetic services to Christ are no more than the "gifts which the first light of its dawn brought to me," as he puts it in that same letter. At the same time, in this giving back, he is not just seeking to articulate the truth of the Christian faith compellingly but striving for superiority over all classical literature.

As he was composing the nativity ode, Milton already imagined himself writing a heroic epic poem like *Paradise Lost*. Thirty-eight years later, when that poem was finally written, he put it on par with anything from Homer or Virgil. One small detail speaks eloquently of his outsized assessment of his own achievement. When *Paradise Lost* was originally published in 1667, it was printed with line numbers in the margins. After noting how unusual, even unique, that was, John Rogers comments,

> The only precedent Milton would have had even for the *idea* of line numbers would have been the great ancient classics, the magnificent Renaissance editions of Homer and Virgil. They would have appeared in the seventeenth century with line numbers because line numbers obviously facilitate the production of scholarly commentary and facilitate the study of those texts in the classroom.

Rogers concludes that Milton intended to "make his poem canonical just like *The Iliad* and just like *The Odyssey* and *The Aeneid* before anyone had actually read it."[37]

Milton seems to have thought that *Paradise Lost* was not just equal to Homer's and Virgil's masterpieces but superior to them. Referring to the authors of those Greek and Latin texts a few years later in *Paradise Regained*, he complains:

> Alas! What can they teach, and not mislead;
> Ignorant of themselves, of God much more,
> And how the world began, and how man fell
> Degraded by himself, on grace depending? *(PR* 4:309–12)

Since *The Iliad, The Odyssey,* and *The Aeneid* were "misleading" their readers about the most important matters—regarding God, sin, and God's grace—they were in that sense inferior to his own work. Perhaps Milton would argue that they were likewise inferior from a poetic standpoint. But in taking pains to point out this comparison, Milton seems to show that he was interested not just in the excellences of truth or poetic craft. Throughout his entire life he seemed to be striving for superiority, even superiority over the greatest competitors, and to have this superiority recognized and recorded in the sight of all. It is one thing to be concerned with the truth and brilliance of one's own works; it is quite another to set up the great classical epics as rivals. Whether his two poems are better than Homer's or Virgil's creations is a question he would have been better off not asking, and certainly better off not asking his readers to ask. In chapters 4 and 5, I will show Paul arguing against glorying in one's comparative advantages.

In *Paradise Regained,* one of Satan's temptations is to induce Jesus to make himself "famous / By wisdom" *(PR* 4:221), which presumably requires publicly displaying his own wisdom as superior to the wisdom contained in Greek classical literature. In response, Milton imagines Jesus insisting that he knows Greek wisdom, that he received the "light from above, from the fountain of light" *(PR* 4:289), which is better than "Nature's light," which the Greeks had *(PR* 4:228). Jesus is making comparative judgments and claims that his kind of wisdom is superior—of greater excellence. Yet Jesus refuses to do what Satan wants him to do—he rejects the invitation to demonstrate publicly that his wisdom is superior in order to elevate himself, in order to be recognized as superior in that way. As in the nativity ode, the God who arrived as

91

an infant in a stable is clearly not after fame and superiority, even though his power and wisdom are in fact superior. But the claim "I am the greatest!" is from the evil one. Milton affirms this, for he argues compellingly in both poems against striving for superiority. And yet, unlike Jesus, he could not always resist temptation.[38]

A truly great poetic work against striving for superiority was born out of its author's own struggle with that very vice. This only seems like a paradox. Everything excellent flows from a sullied human spring. In Milton's view, except in the case of God and the unfallen angels, there is no other kind of spring from which it could flow.

# 4

# "Outdo One Another
in Showing Honor" (Paul)

I n *The Religion of the Earliest Churches*, Gerd Theissen argues that the love of neighbor and the renunciation of status
were the two most basic values of the early Christian ethic—
foundational meta-values, in fact, for all other ethical injunctions.
In one form or another, early Christians shared the value of love of
neighbor with non-Christians, both Jews and gentiles. But renunciation of status and humility were more novel, notwithstanding
certain precedents for them among the Cynic philosophers[1]—and,
as I will show in chapter 6, in the Hebrew Bible as well. The two
virtues pushed against the culture of ancient Rome, in which status, both ascribed and acquired, was paramount.

In the Christian Bible, the most consistent critique of striving
for superiority and the most compelling alternative to such striving are found in the writings of the apostle Paul. Though he was
not the only among the earliest Christian writers concerned with
the issue, he wrote about it more extensively and comprehensively
than any other. A critique of striving for superiority is at the very

core of Paul's deepest concern. Under many more diverse names than strictly "superiority," it comes up in all the autobiographical passages of his writings; in his theologies of creation, salvation, and the church; and in many sections of his letters containing ethical instructions. Importantly, the problems with striving for superiority were among the reasons why he, an ardent Pharisee (in the non-pejorative sense) and a precocious student of the Torah and the traditions, became a committed disciple of Jesus Christ. As he describes it, this life-altering shift in basic orientation was a result of revelation (Gal. 1:11–16). One way to describe the effect of Jesus Christ on Paul—an uncommon and rather formal one but true and, for our purposes, important—is to say that, whatever else allegiance to Christ did in his life, it altered the nature of his striving: from a zealous seeking of superiority to an equally zealous pursuit of a certain kind of excellence. Paul describes it in almost exactly these terms in Philippians 3:3–16 (note v. 4b), as I will try to show shortly.[2]

As I explore the problem of striving for superiority in Paul, I will draw on—and try to unite—two strands of Pauline scholarship. The main one is the classical theological concern about grace and merit, about the nature of human agency and its significance in the justification of human beings before God. This is where the origins of Paul's resistance to striving for superiority lie. The other strand, subsidiary in my project here, is more recent scholarship about Paul's relation to the status-conscious Roman culture into which he was speaking and in which, as Cicero put it, "once we have glimpsed, as it were, some part of [honor's] radiance, there is nothing we are not prepared to bear and suffer in order to secure it."[3]

I will start with Paul's moral instruction and then explore his understanding of the character of God as revealed in the story of Jesus Christ to try to understand why Paul regards striving for any kind of superiority—social, material, moral, or spiritual—as inimical to the gospel message. Then I will look at how these ideas shape Paul's self-understanding and his core teaching of justification by faith. In the next chapter I will explore how Paul deploys this critique of striving for superiority in more polemical contexts.

### 1

Consider three versions of Paul's moral instruction about honoring others in a local community of faith.

First, 1 Corinthians includes an emphatic, albeit indirect, command about honoring others. It is implicit in the way Paul develops an image to illustrate how members of a community should relate to one another. As many before and after him, Paul likens a community to a human body. To those who feel inferior—"Because I am not a hand, I do not belong to the body" (12:15)—he says that they are essential; the body needs them in order to be a body. To those who feel superior and want independence—an eye says to a hand "I have no need of you" (12:21)—he tells them that, in their sense of superiority, they are unduly inflating their value; a single-member body would be grotesque. So far, Paul's account of a community as a body is as one might have expected: the stress is on interdependence and cooperation.

Continuing his argument against the "superior" members (those who glory in their seemingly higher rank, set themselves apart, and disdain those below them), Paul elevates the importance of the weak and "dishonorable" members. Rhetorically, this is where he places the emphasis in the entire section on the body and its members (1 Cor. 12:14–26).

> On the contrary, the members of the body that seem to be weaker are indispensable, and those members of the body that we think less honorable we clothe with greater honor, and our less respectable members are treated with greater respect, whereas our more respectable members do not need this. But God has so arranged the body, giving the greater honor to the inferior member, that there

may be no dissension within the body, but the members may have the same care for one another. (12:22–25)

Paul makes a radical point: against the seeming implications of relative standing on the commonly accepted superiority/inferiority scale, all members ought to have matching honor and "the same care for one another."

In this passage, he is returning to the problem he addressed in chapter 11. The rich, powerful, and high-status members of the church are treating the poor, weak, and "dishonorable" members with disdain and utter lack of care.[4] He writes that at their meetings, during the Lord's Supper, "each of you proceeds to eat your own supper, and one goes hungry and another becomes drunk." The powerful "show contempt for the church of God and humiliate those who have nothing" (1 Cor. 11:21–22). Paul's first argument against them is from the character of the Lord's Supper. It celebrates Christ, who shared himself to the point of death with others. Those who set themselves apart in selfish disdain of others at the Lord's Table, of all places, contradict the very foundation of the church of Christ—and "eat and drink judgment against themselves" (11:29).

As he develops the metaphor of the body, Paul mounts a second argument against the disdainful "superior" members of the church. He states the first and most important step in his argument almost as a side remark. The "less respectable" members of the body only *appear* to be as such in a twisted, "fleshly" way of thinking. The weak, those who have nothing, are being inferiorized: they "*seem* to be weaker" (1 Cor. 12:22) and we "*think* [of them as] less honorable" (12:23)—but in fact they are not. The rich and honored should not confuse worldly appearances with divinely established realities. In the body of the church, *all* are equally honorable, which is why "we clothe with greater honor" those members who appear "less honorable" (12:23). Instead of disdaining seemingly less respectable members and caring only for themselves, the powerful and "distinguished" should treat them with *greater* respect, corresponding to the equal care they ought to show for all members of the body. Honor is equal, and therefore *honoring* should be differentiated in a way that manifests that equality! I will return to this pattern of differential honoring that challenges unequal worldly standards of honor throughout this chapter.

In the political rhetoric of Paul's time, the metaphor of the body was used to justify differences in standing and treatment.[5] In marked contrast, Paul uses it to push for greater equality in honor and care. Imbalance in honor and care given and received creates division within the body. Seeking honor primarily for oneself— striving for superiority—will set equally honorable members who should care for one another in competition for honor with one another. So also will a more passive presumption of one's own superiority and the consequent expectation of uneven distribution of honor and care that comes to one's benefit. Though Paul never urges inferiorized members to struggle for equal honor and care, he himself struggles on their behalf!

As Paul sees it, the vision of equal honor and care is not a mere social convention. This is how *God* has arranged bodies—ecclesial, and more broadly human, communities (1 Cor. 12:24). The moral requirement of equal honor is rooted in human ontology. Human beings are not self-defined sovereign individuals nor persons whose value depends on how they appear in the eyes of others; instead, God, in being their creator, establishes their value, which other humans ought to honor. Neither are they independent individuals whose relation to others depends merely on the will of all involved; they are part of a social body such that the very being, let alone well-being, of each is bound up with the entire social body. "If one member suffers, all suffer together with it; if one member is honored, all rejoice together with it," Paul concludes the paragraph, inviting the joy of each—a shared joy—in the honor given to others (12:26).

When I turn to Paul's theologies of salvation and creation, I will show even more basic ways in which he pushes against the sovereignty of the self. There, too, his purpose is to undercut striving for superiority.

=== ⚎ ===

The second instruction concerning honor in the community is direct and, in a sense, asks of the community more than the first: not just to work for equality of honor but to lead in striving for it. "Outdo one another in showing honor" (Rom. 12:10b). Again, the context is the community as a social body (12:4–5). The stress on both mutual and equal care is also present, only it is now expressed in the language of love: "Love one another with mutual affection" (12:10a). The injunction to mutual honoring, then, does not concern a status hierarchy but the way mutual affection leads one to treat others. He assumes that the honor conferred on others, understood as "a high regard and esteem," is genuine—that it is not the "simulated and mercenary" kind of honor a person confers only in order that they may "receive a greater return," as Martin Luther puts it in his *Lectures on Romans*.[6] Similarly, care for others, the benefits a person confers on them, must not be intended to enhance the honor of the benefactor, as in Roman honor-obsessed culture.

Along with many others, Martin Luther thinks that, for Paul in this passage, honoring another person is based on a comparative judgment of worth: they are more *worthy* of honor than I am, so I honor them rather than refuse to give them the honor due or falsely assert my own greater honor over them. This is because Luther believes that "a man cannot show this honor to another unless he humbles himself and judges *himself worthy* of being put to shame and that *others are more deserving* of honor than he is, that is, unless a man is humble, he does not prefer another in honor above himself."[7] According to this view, honor has to do with exclusive status rankings; to honor another is to move oneself down the list. But that cannot be right, either about humility or about honoring others.

Paul insists on *mutual* honoring, with every member of the community involved. If each person judges others as more *deserving* of honor, then many judgments will simply be false.[8] He insists that each member ought to aspire to think of themselves with "sober," truthful judgment, according to which some will presumably be better in many respects than others (Rom. 12:3)— an injunction Paul makes to push against both those who tend to inflate their self-image (feeling superior and thinking they are more deserving) *and* those who think that to honor another must mean to degrade their own worth or achievements. The conferral of honor upon others cannot therefore be indexed to the merit of each, to what each deserves (see also below).[9] Instead, each ought to be honored irrespective of their merit or demerit, based on the sheer fact of being a member of the ecclesial community and, more broadly, of the human race.

The instruction to "outdo one another in showing honor" (Rom. 12:10) seems, though, not to curb striving for superiority but to put it on its head—and then boost it. Instead of seeking to be superior to others in honors obtained, one ought to seek to be superior in honors conferred. The result would be a kind of moral meritocracy, a striving for moral superiority. That is one possible reading of the text, and this is how some commentators read other passages in Paul, notably Philippians 2:9–11 and 2 Corinthians 11:23–33.[10] In their view, Paul is against striving for superiority only when it aims at power, wealth, and such rather than at love for others and honoring of others. One *should* strive to be superior to others in loving and elevating others, such interpreters of Paul maintain. Aiming at superiority is not the problem, only aiming at superiority with respect to the wrong things.

This interpretation, in my view, is beset by fatal incongruities. It would be like reasoning that, since humility is a cardinal virtue for Christians, one could legitimately take pride in one's humility, glorying in being humbler than one's competitors. In both cases the focus remains on comparisons and contrastive evaluations, not on the pursuit of moral excellence itself. In Romans 12:10, the word translated with "outdo" is *proēgoumenoi* and can be rendered as "leading the way," which fits better in Paul's larger argument than does "beating in competition." This implies, Luther notes, that "we must give honor to one another even if honor given to us from the other person neither precedes nor follows."[11]

Crucial, though, is mutuality—in the sense not of conditional reciprocity but of unconditional dependencies and obligations of each member to every other, what some have called "one-anotherness."[12] Both unconditional care and unconditional honoring of the other should be mutual. Such mutuality in both love and honoring destabilizes social hierarchy. Each ought to show honor irrespective of whether they are being honored or of whether the one they are honoring *merits* honor; this expectation is placed not only on the "inferior" but also, and with greater force, on the "superior"—those who have more wealth or power or are more highly regarded. The primary critical thrust of the command that love and honor be mutual is against those who might be tempted to think of themselves as "superior," whether because they are treated as superior outside the church or because they are moral virtuosos or community leaders.

≡ III ≡

Paul's third command to honor one another is the most radical: "Do nothing from selfish ambition or empty conceit, but in humility regard others as better than yourselves" (Phil. 2:3). This is the most direct rejection of striving for superiority anywhere in Paul. "Better than" (*hyperechontas*) or "superior to" can be taken to refer to either the endowments and accomplishments of others or their standing or importance. As in Romans 12:10, here, too, superiority in endowments and accomplishments can hardly be in view because the "holding to be superior" is to be mutual and unconditional. Every member would have to regard every other member as better than they are, and many would then be making false claims. It is better, then, to interpret *hyperechontas* as "superior in standing or importance," a position that also fits more closely the example of Christ that Paul is about to give: by serving them, the one equal with God holds even the lowliest humans to be superior in importance to himself.

The members of the Christian community in Philippi—*all* of them—should not seek to assert their own self-worth and importance either through rivalry with others (*eritheian*: selfish ambition) or by seeking to please others to receive their praise (*kenodoxian*: vainglory). Instead, in humble self-forgetfulness, each should regard others as more important than themselves—or rather, since all others in fact have equal standing and importance, they should relate to and treat them *as if* they have higher standing and importance.[13] Which members of the community should the Philippians honor as their superiors? All of them, "without restriction," answers Karl Barth, commenting on the verse.[14] Each person treating every other person as more important might be the most effective way to establish equality of honor in communities in which some are falsely deemed inferior and others falsely deemed superior.

As the metaphor of the body has been used both to argue for the importance of hierarchical relations and to challenge them (as Paul uses it in 1 Cor. 12), so too the injunction to mutual honoring can be deployed in different ways. If, for example, it is directed mostly at those who are lower, or if "to honor someone" is taken to mean according them the treatment due their social rank, then it can solidify existing status relations.[15] Pushing against the humiliation of the poor during the Lord's Supper, in 1 Corinthians 12, Paul argues that honoring should *not* be equal but that the poor should receive greater honor—so that honor is equalized among members. He also stresses *equal* care, which presumably means that the rich should share some of their wealth with the poor.

In Philippians 2, honoring others means actively looking after their interests: "Let each of you look not to your own interests but [also] to the interests of others" (v. 4)[16]—and therefore does not solidify existing status relations. In relating to others, the one who strives for superiority over another looks out, above all, for their own interests, to outdo others if they are deemed superior or not to lose their superior position if they are deemed inferior. In contrast, those who hold others higher than themselves attend primarily to the interests of others (though to do so, their own selves have to be secured in other ways than by self-assertion over others, as I will explore shortly). Here, too, Paul is after mutuality. If each ought to look out for the good of others and if each holds others as higher than themselves, then every giver and every recipient will all together form a community of "giving and receiving," to borrow Paul's phrase from 4:15. If the members who are "higher" or materially better off truly look out for the interests of those who are lower, then the scales of superiority will be destabilized, not entrenched.

In all three passages I have analyzed—each from a different letter but each part of instruction about the life of church communities —Paul rejects striving for superiority and urges his readers to honor one another as they would someone of equal or superior standing. In commenting on the passage from Philippians, Karl Barth asks, On what grounds should one relate to others as if they had higher standing? "Not on this ground or that, perhaps *without* any grounds, *counter* to every ground,"[17] he answers, implying that such honoring of others is neither based on their merit nor obstructed by their demerit. It is grounded in their mere humanity, shared by every human being equally, a point I also showed Kierkegaard emphasizes (chap. 2). The main reason for honoring each person more than oneself, rather than striving for superiority, and the reason for the radical social vision is the story of Jesus Christ. "Have this mind among yourselves, which is yours in Christ Jesus," Paul writes (Phil. 2:5 RSV). What immediately follows is the famous hymn to Christ (2:6–11).

Reading the story of Jesus Christ as a sketch of the pattern one's life ought to take, we need to keep in mind that, though Paul urges his readers to act like Christ, imitation is not his main point; he is not merely giving moral instruction. As I will show in the section after next, for Paul, living in conformity with the Christ comes about because the resurrected Christ, embraced by faith, becomes the main acting agent of a person's life. He is inviting his readers to union with Christ.

## 2

In *Reconstructing Honor in Roman Philippi*, Joseph Hellerman argues that in ancient Roman colonies, as in Rome, honor was paramount. A common path to glory involved coming to occupy an ascending order of offices. This was known as the *cursus honorum* (race of honors). He proposes that the story of Jesus Christ told in Philippians 2:6–8—the so-called Carmen Christi—is about a very different race, a *cursus pudorum* (race of shames). Teresa Morgan expresses doubt over whether the strict *cursus honorum* was particularly important in Rome at the time of Paul and whether it was practiced in Philippi.[18] If we take the *cursus honorum* in a more general sense, however—as an ascending path of achieving honors—we may still contrast it with the way the Carmen Christi renders the story of Christ.

Referring to Jesus Christ, to whom Christians ought to conform themselves, Paul writes:

> who, though he existed in the form of God,
>     did not regard equality with God
>     as something to be grasped,
> but emptied himself,

> taking the form of a slave,
> assuming human likeness.
> And being found in appearance as a human,
>   he humbled himself
>   and became obedient to the point of death—
>   even death on a cross. (Phil. 2:6–8)

Each stanza describes a step of Christ's *loss* of status. Hellerman writes,

> Paul's portrayal of Jesus consists in three progressively degrading positions of social status in the Roman world. . . . Jesus descends in *cursus pudorum* from equality with God (Status Level One), through the taking on of humanity and the status of a slave (Status Level Two), to the public humiliation of death on the cross (Status Level Three).[19]

Jesus Christ starts at the very top on the honor scale: "he existed in the form of God." As I read this complex text—about which a whole library has been written—the "form of God" is God in outward appearance. One can appear in the form of God, appear in divine glory, only if one *is* God or equal to God, which is what the hymn indirectly asserts: Christ "did not count equality with God [which he had] a thing to be grasped" (Phil. 2:6 ESV). The claim that Christ is equal to God is a claim to the highest possible metaphysical status; if one is not God, one can neither become equal to God by one's own striving nor, obviously, strive to retain the status of equality with God. Kings and rulers in Hellenistic and Roman traditions sought to usurp equality with God, wielding it as an instrument for maintaining the highest superiority and exercising uncontested rule. In Milton, as I have shown, Satan starts a war in heaven and wreaks havoc on earth because he strives to make himself God's superior (chap. 3). All these are examples of grasping after and publicly asserting equality with God, which, in the context of monotheism, can only mean dethroning God and placing oneself on God's throne.

104

The contrast to usurpation of equality is not that Jesus did not aspire to equality with God but that he did not regard his equality as something to be held graspingly and exploited to his own benefit.[20] In the incarnation, he gave up not equality with God but the form of God, the outward appearance of divinity that would manifest his superiority to humanity and legitimize his rule, a point Kierkegaard emphasizes in his use of Philippians 2 (see chap. 2).[21] In his great and decisive descent, Christ took off the garment of divine glory—God as the pinnacle of superiority—taking on the form of a slave, and then ending up on the cross. From the vantage point of aspirations to honor, this was the ultimate ignominy. As God, he became human; as human, he took the form of a slave; as slave, he was obedient to the point of death. And the death to which he willingly went was the most shameful execution of all.[22]

The assumption of the hymn is that Christ's self-emptying was not a mere show of some paradoxically heroic self-debasement. He humbled himself utterly to serve others, to do for others what they were unable to do for themselves. In fact, as the universalist scope of Philippians 2:9–11—"every knee" everywhere—suggests, he died in shame on behalf of the whole of humanity, perhaps especially on behalf of the most despised of slaves, whose lives sometimes ended on the cross as his did. Here, then, we have the extreme, and for mere humans unattainable, form of the stance Paul is exhorting the Philippian Christians to take. Jesus Christ, the one with actual unmatched status, acted most radically *as if* even the least important human and the gravest sinner were superior to him. He looked out for their interests rather than his own (2:3–4). And he did so not because of their merits but irrespective of any of their demerits and regardless of his own equality with the Most High.

═══ ⫫ ═══

After Philippians 2:8, there is a sharp break in the hymn to Christ. Christ's willing journey downward ends in death on the cross. From

105

verse 9 on, he is no longer an agent of his own story. God the Father is, and God's action is linked with an emphatic "therefore" to the stages of self-emptying of which verses 6 to 8 speak.

> Therefore God also highly exalted him
> and gave him the name
> that is above every name,
> so that at the name of Jesus
> every knee should bend,
> in heaven and on earth and under the earth,
> and every tongue should confess
> that Jesus Christ is Lord,
> to the glory of God the Father. (2:9–11 NRSV)

One way to understand the link between the two parts of the poem—"therefore"—is to think of the exaltation as the reward for Christ's self-abasement. On this reading, the way to get to the highest honor is, counterintuitively, to run the *cursus pudorum* instead of, as one would expect, the *cursus honorum*. This is Hellerman's position: "As a reward for dishonoring himself for the benefit of others, Jesus is exalted to the highest place by One" who is "at the very apex of the pecking order of social reality."[23] If this is correct, we would return to a form of the moral meritocracy that some interpreters find in Romans 12:10. One would remain within the cultural frame of shame and honor. Both "shame" and "honor" would retain their meaning, but the *way* to honor would be different because the direction of the *cursus* is reversed. Instead of running from low to high, one would run from high to low, and God would, in the final reversal, elevate one as victor in reward. God then confers honor on those who do dishonorable service—arduous, painful, shameful, slavish—for the benefit of others. The reward is extrinsic to the work, like money for sweat. Friedrich Nietzsche's "Luke 18:14 improved" would then be vindicated: "He who humbles himself wants to be exalted."[24]

It seems more consistent with the entire story, however—and with Paul's claim in 1 Corinthians 2:8 that the "rulers of this age" have crucified "the Lord of glory"—to think that, with the exaltation of the crucified Jesus Christ, his entire downward journey was declared to be exalted. This kind of love is itself glorious; God's exaltation publicly vindicates this truth rather than rewarding Christ with some other glory besides that of the radical love he practiced. With respect to Christ's relation to the fallen and needy world, the glory of Christ consists not in striving to maintain divine eminence nor in exploiting it to control others but in acting for the benefit of others: in taking on the form of a despised slave and dying a shameful death. Jesus Christ was no less God, and therefore no less exalted, at the lowest point of his *cursus pudorum* than he was either before the journey or after the Father placed him into the highest public honor. I don't mean that God's exaltation of Christ is a mere declaration that Christ's deed, generally considered shameful, is glorious.[25] Exaltation raises the crucified Christ himself into the new life of glory that, as the Son, he had before the foundation of the world.

Giving the raised Christ the name above all names—the holy name of God—is a public proclamation that all creatures should worship as their Lord the One sitting on the single throne with God who took on the form of a slave and died on the cross. In his downward journey, Jesus Christ demonstrated what it means to be the Most High—when faced with the fragility and need of creatures.[26] As Martin Luther puts it in "The Magnificat," "For since He [God] is the Most High, and there is nothing above Him, He cannot look above Him; nor to either side, for there is none like him. He must needs, therefore look within Him and beneath Him; and the farther one is beneath Him, the better does He see him."[27] This kind of loving "seeing" is God's glory.

≡ ⫯⫯⫯ ≡

Philippians 2 is not the story of an *increase* in superiority—of Christ's striving to increase his standing by public proclamation of his divine glory and its recognition by all creatures, earthly and heavenly. If it were the story of striving for superiority, he would be too close for comfort to Satan in the story that Milton, inspired by the hymn to Christ in Philippians, tells in *Paradise Lost* (see chap. 3). More importantly, if the one who went on a downward journey to the cross was God, he does not need his glory increased because he already is as glorious as could be. Paul composed (or reproduced) the hymn to Christ to motivate Christians in Philippi not to strive to outdo one another in honor but to regard one another as if others were more important than themselves, to look to the interests of others and not primarily their own (Phil. 2:3–4). Christ's own journey both exemplifies the morally excellent way that is worthy of human striving and gives assurance that such striving will result not in shame and death but in resurrection and exaltation with Christ. "He will transform the body of our humiliation," Paul writes one chapter later in Philippians, "that it may be conformed to the body of his glory" (3:21).

**3**

Mutually loving and honoring others more than oneself in acts of humble service is the way of life (*politheuomai*) in the alternative polity that is the church (Phil. 1:27). Jesus Christ, its Lord, is the model of just this kind of life, Paul reminds the Philippians. In the letter to them, Paul tells of the stark difference this new way of life has made in his own biography. Examining this more closely will help us understand the central role the critique of striving for superiority plays in Paul's thought.

———iii———

In Philippians 3:2–6, Paul gives an account of his former life, similar to the one we find in Galatians 1:13–14. In both, striving for superiority is an important concern.

> If anyone has a reason to be confident in the flesh, I have more:
> circumcised on the eighth day, a member of the people of Israel, of
> the tribe of Benjamin, a Hebrew born of Hebrews; as to the law, a
> Pharisee; as to zeal, a persecutor of the church; as to righteousness
> under the law, blameless. (Phil. 3:4–6)

"If anyone has . . . I have more!" As this opening boast suggests,
the passage is part of a larger polemic. The way of Christ is threatened, Paul believes, not just by striving for superiority outside the
church—by the culture of honor—but by striving for superiority
within the church. False preachers promoted a vision of Christian
life as an alternative form of *cursus honorum* (in a more general
sense of the phrase).

There is a version of striving for superiority that is set outside
any moral order. In Paul's social environment, it was about superiority in honor based largely on political power. But there is also
a version of striving for superiority that takes place within a moral
order, a *cursus honorum* based on religious and moral standing
and achievement. (Kierkegaard pushes strenuously against this
kind of striving for superiority, as I noted in chap. 2.) As Paul sees
it, that's how some of the Christian communities understand the
way of Christ: striving for moral and religious superiority, with
circumcision as a special mark of belonging. With anger flashing
in his eyes, he describes these preachers as "dogs," "evil workers,"
and "those who mutilate the flesh." And before each term of dis-
approbation he exclaims, "Beware!" (Phil. 3:2).

(We need to tread carefully here. Paul's more general relation
to Judaism is too complicated of a topic to address in a text that
is focused on striving for superiority. As I have noted briefly and
will return to in more depth, pushing against claims to superiority
is a key feature of Judaism's defining texts (chap. 6). My sense is
that Paul here is pushing against what he sees to be a *perversion* of
Judaism: the perversion represented by his own former mistaken
ways of living.)

In the quick succession of his own religious "badges," we can still feel Paul's anger, both at the false teachers and at his own former self. He places the badges on his chest just to tear them off and throw them into the garbage bin. Before his encounter with Christ, he was engaged in the quest for moral and religious superiority through obedience to God's law, and these badges were proof of his superior achievement! Paul's list covers two kinds of honors social scientists have identified: ascribed honors (those he inherited at birth by virtue of belonging to a chosen people) and acquired honors (those that were his by virtue of his own achievements).[28] Hellerman notes that, in colonial Philippi, as in imperial Rome, the two types of honors were everywhere listed in just the order in which Paul puts them.[29] If so, Paul projects his advance in Judaism onto the progression of the *cursus honorum*, implying that the two are varieties of the same striving for superiority.

Paul puts his striving for religious advancement in explicitly competitive terms: he has more reason to boast than "anyone." This is hyperbole, just as his claim that he was blameless as to the righteousness according to the law is hyperbole, which must be hyperbole if he still believes, as he does in Romans 3:20, that no "flesh" is able to obey the law fully. He writes in the character of a striver for superiority whose terminal goal can only be to be the best. In a less emotionally charged autobiographical section in Galatians, he notes, more accurately, that he "advanced in Judaism beyond many in my people of the same age, for I was far more zealous for the traditions of my ancestors" (Gal. 1:14). No superlatives, but still a boast about being superior: "beyond many" and "far more." This suggests that his motive was not simply zeal for God—which he explicitly encourages members of his churches to have (in Rom. 12:11, right after the injunction for each to lead in showing honor to others!)—but also his own elevated standing among his peers.[30]

Paul believed he had good reasons for confidence in the flesh. Both his ascribed and his achieved standings were superior. In striving for complete obedience to God's law, he was competing—and winning. Yet, he writes, after completing the list of achievements, "whatever gains I had, these I have come to regard as loss" (Phil. 3:7)—worse than loss, as "rubbish," underscoring that what purportedly gave him superior standing not only had lost all value but also had been exposed as having negative value. Now, the *fact* that he was "a Hebrew born of Hebrews" had not become rubbish, for he still believed that to the Hebrews "belong the adoption, the glory, the covenants, the giving of law, and the promises" and that from them came, "according to the flesh . . . the Christ, who is over all, God blessed forever" (Rom. 9:4–5). Similarly, the *fact* that he was righteous according to the law (to the extent that he was) had also not become rubbish, for he believed that "the law is holy, and the commandment ["You shall not covet"] is holy and just and good" (7:12). Finally, the *fact* that he was zealous had not become rubbish, though his zeal in persecuting the church was rubbish, for he continued to run hard as a follower and an apostle of Jesus Christ; even the undercurrent of anger as he is writing about the gain that has turned to loss bears witness to his zeal.

Without ceasing to be positive, what had been positive for Paul has turned negative, become rubbish. How? He had made these great goods of his ancestry, zeal, and achievements *into* rubbish by directing them toward inappropriate and unworthy goals. He was using them to secure righteousness before God, and they had proven inadequate for that (see sec. 4). But he was using them also to "boast in himself," to feel superior, and to claim superiority. They were a means to elevate himself above others, to diminish—inferiorize—others, even to persecute some of them. To turn these good things into means of self-elevation is, in a sense, already to treat them as rubbish, as worthless in themselves. This turning to rubbish is the effect of striving for superiority on many goods, moral values and ordinary goods of life, as Kierkegaard and Milton noted (chaps. 2 and 3).

———※———

There is, however, a striving that aims at what is truly worthwhile. Paul describes the object of his new striving as "the superiority [*hyperechon*] of knowing Christ Jesus my Lord" (Phil. 3:8, author's translation). "Superiority" is a startling and puzzling word here, and I'll get to it in a moment. To understand it properly, we need to know what he means by "knowing." It is primarily a matter not of the intellect but of the self's entire orientation. Paul is striving to know Jesus Christ as *his* Lord. "Lord" is a common title for Jesus Christ in Paul's writings, but when it appears here, early in Philippians 3, it is hard not to hear in it echoes of the end of the hymn to Christ from the previous chapter: "and every tongue should confess that Jesus Christ is Lord" (2:11). The one who was equal to God, who became a slave and died on the cross, and whom God exalted—*that* one is Paul's Lord, the goal of his striving. The knowledge of him is superior to all other knowledge. "I want to know Christ and the power of his resurrection and the sharing of his sufferings by becoming like him [*symmorphizomenos*] in his death, if somehow I may attain the resurrection from the dead" (3:10–11).

Christ's journey begins with his status as God's equal. Analogously, Paul's new life begins with resurrection. Baptismal experience is what makes this first step possible. Paul has been crucified with Christ and raised with Christ into new life, the life of the resurrected Christ in him (Rom. 6:3–4; Gal. 2:19–20). This transformation constitutes his new self with a new way of life. But the power of the resurrected Christ leads him not to glory—or, rather, not *straight* to glory—as ordinarily understood, but on a journey downward, like the foundational and paradigmatic journey Christ undertook. Leaning on the dialectic of lordship and servanthood that Martin Luther sketches in *The Freedom of the Christian*, we can put it this way: established by being raised with Christ to be a "lord," the new self becomes a servant and takes the form of (*symmorphizomenos*: conformed to) the earthly Christ, serving others, relating to them as if they were superior (*hyperechontas*), and looking to their interests more than to one's own (Phil. 3:10; 2:3–4).[31] Paul is striving after conformity with Christ—to make Christ "his own" as Christ had made Paul "his own" (Phil. 3:12–13)—in hope (*ei pōs*: if somehow) that he will be raised from the dead into glory as Jesus Christ was (3:11). It may seem, then, that the ultimate goal of striving is not conformity to Christ but the reward of resurrection. Not likely. Paul is identifying with the entire journey of Christ. More importantly, it is Christ, glorious in his suffering for others and in his exaltation, who is not just the goal of his striving but its acting agent.[32] Such "knowledge" of Christ, the life like Christ's that he lives by Christ living in him, Paul considers superior to life according to human standards. In 1 Corinthians, he calls this kind of knowledge of Christ the "wisdom of God" (1:24) and deems it "wiser than human wisdom" (1:25). Such knowledge of Christ is also superior to all his achievements, and in light of it he came to count his achievements as loss (Phil. 3:8).

The superiority that Paul embraces and that he believes he can have without striving to be superior to anyone is the superiority of Christ—his person, his way, and his agency in human lives. It is a superiority not achieved but given to everyone ready to receive it.

≡ ⫶⫶⫶ ≡

Is not conformity to Christ just another way to strive for superiority, though, to be able to boast not in some dazzling success but in one's self-decentering service? Maybe it's like that variant interpretation of Romans 12:10 I argued against above, as if Paul were saying, "Outcompete one another in knowing Christ!" Is it that only the object of striving is now different—not the greatness of the law and righteousness before the law but conformity to the suffering and dying Christ—and the ultimate goal of striving (namely, superiority over others) remains the same? This would be a misreading of Paul. In Philippians 3:4–6, Paul implicitly rejects striving for superiority, even striving to be better than others in morally admirable qualities and achievements. He thinks that Christ's superiority does not redound to his own superiority to others. But has he remained consistent?

A few verses later in Philippians, and elsewhere as well (for instance, 1 Cor. 9:24–27), Paul uses sports metaphors to describe his reaching toward the new goal: "forgetting what lies behind and straining forward to what lies ahead, I press on toward the goal" (Phil. 3:13–14). He is going for the "prize" (3:14). Does that not imply that he is competing again, trying to beat others to the prize? It would seem so in 1 Corinthians, where he explicitly states, "In a race the runners all compete, but only one receives the prize" (9:24). And yet it would be wrong to conclude that he is striving to best *others*. When he applies the race analogy to the Christian life, the idea of one person alone getting the prize completely disappears: "Run in such a way that you may win" (9:24). The "you" here is grammatically plural: all of you should run in a way that each of you wins, which, in this race, is both possible and desirable. The goal is universally accessible and not exclusive; therefore, all can win. In Paul's use of a sports analogy in 1 Corinthians, Christian ministry and life require intense effort, discipline, and focus. Similarly, in Philippians, as Paul strives for conformity with Christ, he wants his readers to strive for the same thing (Phil. 3:15)—with the discipline and focus of an athlete. But the success of one does not require the failure of all others.[33]

In Philippians 3:7–14, striving for superiority gives way to striving for a certain kind of excellence. This excellence, as I will demonstrate, is also a gift, though one that does not exclude striving but encompasses it.

=== ✠ ===

To many people, to all those who judge by "fleshly," commonsense standards, what Paul calls "superior knowledge" looks like foolishness—a self-defeating striving after self-diminishment, even self-sacrifice, rather than an admirable commitment to the well-being of others. Aren't some people better than others? Don't some work harder and achieve more? Do they not, therefore, *deserve* more praise? If so, what could be wrong with striving for greater merit than others and more praise, whether for performing better than others in Christlike service, military conquests, or academic achievements? And why not have confidence in ourselves, in the "flesh," if we have reason for such confidence (Phil. 3:4)? Or if we don't, why not aim to acquire such confidence? Why should we not boast of our superior achievements, to the extent that they are genuine and our account of them truthful? What's so divinely wise about renouncing striving for superiority?

One answer Paul could give is that the Christian community aims for equal honor for each member and the same care for all. But that seems more like an evasion than an answer. Why *should* honor be equal when merit is not? Isn't it, in fact, *unjust* to treat those who are unequal equally? Isn't the principle of justice "equality to equals, inequality to unequals," as Nietzsche puts it in *Twilight of the Idols*? In that case, the rule should be to "never make unequals equal."[34]

Paul encountered some such resistance to his account of the Christian life, as I will suggest in the next chapter. In his view, God's justice challenges this "commonsense" understanding of justice. He insisted, though, that "God's foolishness is wiser than human wisdom, and God's weakness is stronger than human strength" (1 Cor. 1:25). I therefore now turn to his account of the way we are saved by God's seemingly foolish justice—to his central teaching about justification by faith.


# 4

A good way to see how Paul's theology of salvation cuts against striving for superiority is to examine his stance on the practice of boasting, a sense and a public claim that one is superior to others.

Whether in the form of a "humblebrag" or narcissistic bombast, it is a favorite sport of any striver for superiority. Their standing depends not so much on their *being* superior as on others *recognizing* them as superior, a crucial point that I showed Jean-Jacques Rousseau makes in his analysis of the origin of inequality in *amour propre* (see chap. 1). I also showed it concretely exemplified in Milton's striving not just to be better than the great classical poets but to be publicly recognized as such (see chap. 3).

In Philippians, Paul describes the shift in his life after his encounter with Christ as a change in the practice of boasting. A man who had all reason to have "confidence in the flesh" (Phil. 3:4), which is to say, in his own capacities, to secure him superior status before God and who boasted in being (among) the best in his religious practice became a person who, though an exceptional achiever, gave up on confidence in the flesh and came to "boast in Jesus Christ" (3:3). He sees the new version of himself as "not having a righteousness of my own that comes from the law but one that comes through faith in Christ, the righteousness from God based on faith" (3:9). This autobiographical sketch corresponds to his theological position, articulated in Romans, on God's relation to humans and humans' relations to themselves and others.

<hr>

"Then what becomes of boasting?" (Rom. 3:27), Paul asks in the middle of his extended argument in Romans (2:1–4:25). By boasting, he means glorying in both ascribed and achieved status, in being a member of the Jewish people entrusted with the Torah and, especially, in rendering obedience to the Torah.[35] He responds,

> It is excluded. Through what kind of law? That of works? No, rather through the law of faith. For we hold that a person is justified by faith apart from works prescribed by the law. Or is God the God of Jews only? Is he not the God of gentiles also? Yes, of gentiles also, since God is one, and he will justify the circumcised

[the Jews] on the ground of faith and the uncircumcised [the gentiles] through that same faith. (3:27–30)

Since God is one, God is the God of both Jews and gentiles and has the same way of salvation—the same way of life—for all humans. God justifies all "by faith apart from works prescribed by the law" (Rom. 3:28). The righteousness of the justified is not in any sense their own performance; it is God's gift. It comes not from them but "from God," to use the formulation from Philippians 3:9 (cf. 1 Cor. 1:30). Martin Luther calls it "alien righteousness": it belongs to humans but always as God's gift and not as their autonomous or divinely assisted achievement.[36] A sense of superiority on account of such an achievement ("law of works") is therefore excluded. One cannot boast in oneself as the acquirer or possessor of this kind of righteousness, even though it is so intimately one's own that it qualifies one's whole being. One can legitimately boast only in the giver—who turns out to be the one God of all and therefore is not available to anyone as an instrument of striving for superiority over anyone else.

≡ ⁂ ≡

Abraham is the most notable case of a righteous person who had no right to boast. He stands at the very beginning of the history of salvation, and God's relation to him is paradigmatic of God's relation to all humanity. Abraham "believed the LORD, and the LORD reckoned it to him as righteousness" (Gen. 15:6). In ancient Jewish literature about Abraham, "he was declared righteous *subsequent to* and *because of* his obedience," Simon Gathercole writes.[37] In 1 Maccabees 2:55, for instance, Abraham was "found faithful in temptation and it was reckoned to him as righteousness." We also find a similar formulation in the New Testament: "Was not our ancestor Abraham justified by works when he offered his son Isaac on the altar?" (James 2:21). Paul, however, inverts the sequence of obedience and justification, aligning it more closely with Genesis. Abraham was first reckoned righteous due to his trust in God and God's promises (Gen. 15) and then proved faithful in temptation (Gen. 22).

Paul explains the consequence: "Now to one who works, wages are not reckoned as a gift but as something due. But to one who does not work but trusts him who justifies the ungodly, such faith is reckoned as righteousness" (Rom. 4:4–5). The most startling, and in some ways disturbing, word in the text is "ungodly." Was *Abraham* ungodly, an idolater, when God justified him?[38] Or was the fact that he was justified by faith and not by works an indication that God justifies even the ungodly, which he wasn't?[39] Either way, no religious or moral achievement was required as a prerequisite, only trust in God's promise. Was trust not his achievement, then, giving him ground to boast? Paul explicitly denies that Abraham had *any* ground for boasting, which is why Martin Luther considered faith, and not just righteousness, to be the gift of God as well.[40]

But why? Trust or no trust, shouldn't God reward merit and condemn demerit, give everyone their due wages (as Paul explicitly states, in Rom. 2:6), and praise as superior those who work hard and therefore earn much? In the middle of the section in which God appears as the giver of due wages, Paul ends the first part of his argument by claiming that human beings cannot be "justified before him [God] by deeds prescribed by the law" (3:20). The human condition is such that the law, which ought to be obeyed, in the very act of demanding obedience also generates desire for transgression (7:7–11). If God were to command, monitor observance, and then render judgment on whether a person is just or not, no human would be found righteous. If justification is to happen, it is to be not merited self-justification but a gift of God.

For Paul, justification is not a declaration about the existing moral state of a person but a creative act of God, who "calls into existence the things that do not exist" (Rom. 4:17).[41] The way one acquires righteousness and the way one comes into being are analogous. Both are an unconditional divine gift of creation. Righteousness is the result of the gift of "new creation" in virtue of Christ's presence in the believer, as I have shown in the discussion of Paul's own coming to faith in Christ, his dying and rising with Christ. The means by which the self is constituted as righteous precludes ascribing in any way the origin of righteousness to the self. Any claim to have worked oneself into a superior religious or moral status is a self-inflating falsehood.

===⚌===

Let's retrace briefly the road we have traveled. In Romans 3 and 4, Paul explores righteousness *before* God—whether one acquires it through one's effort to obey the law ("work") or whether one receives it as a gift of God ("faith" or, better, "trust"[42]). But receiving the gift of righteousness and "good standing" before God has crucial consequences for the relation between believing Jews and gentiles, undermining the claims to superiority of either group but especially of the gentile Christians (see Rom. 11:17–24). God's oneness implies one way of salvation, exemplified in Abraham, the ancestor of us all: the model of justification by faith (3:29–30; 4:1–12). Later, at the end of Romans, in a chapter about living a life of faith (Rom. 12–16), one implication of received righteousness is the command to "outdo one another in showing honor" (12:10), combined with the command to mutual love (sec. 1).

In Philippians, Paul sketches this critique of works-righteousness in autobiographical terms and sets it explicitly in the context of a polemic against striving for superiority. He also shows that treating others as if they were superior to oneself—as a *mutual* obligation!—is the Christian alternative to striving for superiority, rooted in the story of Christ (secs. 2 and 3).

These are the pillars of Paul's critique of striving for superiority. It is rooted in the humility of Christ and the free grace of God in salvation. It precludes striving for superiority (even moral or religious superiority) and instead gives rise to striving for excellence and a culture of mutual honoring. In the next chapter, I will examine how Paul applies and expands this framework in his writings to a church that found itself beset by teachers who wanted to use Christianity to strive for higher social status, for what they thought was a new and better kind of superiority.

# 5

# "What Do You Have That You Did Not Receive?" (Paul)

In Romans, Paul is writing to a church he has not started and he does not personally know. He introduces himself by sketching the content of his own account of the Christian faith. In Philippians, Paul is writing to a friendly church, his firstborn in Europe, willing to go where he is leading them. He is addressing, in part, quarrels within that church, but these have nothing to do with the Philippians' relation to him. He sketches his alternative to striving for superiority without polemic, except for the polemic against his own former self, a zealous striver for superiority.

In Corinth, some 350 kilometers to the south of Philippi, he is facing a church rebellion against him and internal quarrels in part due to that rebellion. The contending parties identify with a leader in their quarrels. "Each of you says," Paul writes at the beginning of the letter, "'I belong to Paul,' or 'I belong to Apollos,' or 'I belong to Cephas,' or 'I belong to Christ'" (1 Cor. 1:12). The hero of the main party is Apollos, an eloquent teacher of wisdom,

121

and that party is in rebellion against Paul, who, to their disappointment, is not a superior-word (*hyperochēn logou*) preacher of wisdom (2:1–2). He is proclaiming the crucified Christ. To his opponents, Paul's theology of the cross is an ideology of losers, which is how he himself appears to them as well. They want to be winners, preferring a theology of glory (1 Cor. 1:10–4:21).[1] At the center of the difference are their respective assessments of striving for superiority. The members of the parties are "puffed up," as Paul puts it, for being followers of the one and opponents of the other.[2] Boasting about their leader (Apollos) and tearing down the one they deem his competitor (Paul), they are in fact striving for their own superiority, expanding the edges of their own selves with the hot air of their leader's reputation. Paul is determined to put an end to these sectarian tensions arising from striving for superiority.

To argue his case, he leans on arguments from the theology of salvation (sec. 1) and the theology of creation (sec. 2), and he offers reasons why the relation between him and Apollos is one of collaboration rather than competition, as his opponents have assumed (sec. 3). This gives Paul the opportunity to develop new arguments against striving for superiority that are complementary to what we find in his letters to the Romans and the Philippians.

His first letter evidently did not persuade his opponents. In his second letter (2 Cor. 10:1–12:13), his gloves are off and he turns to polemic, comparing himself directly to the leaders he derides as "super-apostles" (sec. 4). The drama of these chapters is not so much whether he will win the Corinthians over but whether he will lose the argument by betraying his own firm opposition to striving for superiority and boasting himself—the original apple of discord. I end the chapter (sec. 5) by reflecting on the challenge that embracing Christ's path and rejecting striving for superiority represents: What would it take for a camel (the striver for superiority) to pass through the eye of a needle and become a follower of Christ?

**1**

From the start, Paul doubles down on his rejection of what he calls worldly standards of superiority. It is the core of who he is as a person and as an apostle. The gospel he proclaims, unapologetically and without eloquent wisdom, can be summed up in one ignominious phrase, a variation of what we know from Philippians 2: the word of the cross (see 1 Cor. 1:17–18). "Christ crucified" is "a stumbling block to Jews," who demand signs, and "foolishness to gentiles," who desire wisdom. To those who are called, however, both Jews and Greeks, that very Christ is "the power of God and the wisdom of God" (1:22–24). Two kinds of power and two kinds of wisdom are clashing: power and wisdom as understood by the present, "fleshly," and therefore perishing age, and power and wisdom as redefined by the crucified Lord. What appears from one perspective as wisdom and strength looks from the other like folly and weakness. Paul is convinced, though, that "God's foolishness is wiser than human wisdom, and God's weakness is stronger than human strength" (1:25). This feels like a competitive claim, but for Paul there is no competition here. He is pointing to the unalterable reality of the relation between Creator and creature, God and flesh (cf. Isa. 40:6). The key question is whether the flesh, which is as ephemeral as grass, can trust the God who appeared "incognito," as Kierkegaard put it,[3] in the folly and weakness of the cross, whether frail humans are able and willing to live in this kind of weakness and folly as long as this present form of the world lasts.

Paul knows that the dissenting party in Corinth is unlikely simply to accept the implications of Christ's weakness. It's what they are rebelling against. Whatever God's intentions might have been with the crucifixion of Jesus Christ, the Corinthians want a God of wisdom and strength, the God of the resurrection—not Paul's humble God of crucifixion, foolish and weak. To make them rethink and realize that the cross is far from irrelevant to the

Christian way of life, Paul appeals to their own social standing when they embraced the gospel he preached.

> Consider your own call, brothers and sisters: not many of you were wise by human standards, not many were powerful, not many were of noble birth. But God chose what is foolish in the world to shame the wise; God chose what is weak in the world to shame the strong; God chose what is low and despised in the world, things that are not, to abolish things that are, so that no one might boast in the presence of God. In contrast, God is why you are in Christ Jesus, who became for us wisdom from God, and righteousness and sanctification and redemption, in order that, as it is written, "Let the one who boasts, boast in the Lord." (1 Cor. 1:26–31)

For Paul, redeeming those who are pushed aside or exploited as inferior—and who often internalize such treatment—is paradigmatic of how God works. His understanding of God's favor to the seemingly inferior stands in the long tradition of the songs of Moses, Miriam, and Hannah in the Hebrew Bible (Exod. 15:1–18, 21; 1 Sam. 2:1–10) and of the song of Mary in the New Testament (Luke 1:46–55). God chooses what is foolish, weak, and despised in worldly terms to shame what is wise, strong, and noble. Put more generally and more radically, God chooses "things that are not, to reduce to nothing things that are" (1 Cor. 1:28 NRSV).

This is the first half of Paul's case, and the Corinthians are likely with Paul up to this point. That's the kind of God worth having, the God who puts to shame those who are deemed by themselves and others to be superior and brings them to nothing. That same God, the Corinthians think, diverging from where Paul is trying to take them, elevates those who are, by ordinary standards, inferior to the position of superiority. That seems to have been the Corinthian theology.[4] From Paul's perspective, though, theirs is an ideology of losers who crave the tables to be turned, an expression of *ressentiment*, as Nietzsche would identify it many centuries later.[5] With biting irony, Paul sketches the social position into which they project themselves with the help of what may be described as "superiority theology":

> Already you have all you want! Already you have become rich! Quite apart from us you have become kings. If only you had become kings, so that we might be kings with you! . . . We are fools for the sake of Christ, but you are sensible people in Christ. We are weak, but you are strong. You are honored, but we are dishonored. (1 Cor. 4:8, 10)

The Corinthians imagine themselves as having already become the ruling nobility with the help of the God whose purpose is their own superior status, the God who chooses "things that are not" (namely, themselves) "to reduce to nothing things that are" (namely, their superiors). The words are Paul's, but as the Corinthians use them, their meaning is the opposite of what Paul intends.

═ ▦ ═

Just at this point, Paul's argument makes a sharp turn—so as to stay on the path of God's journey into foolishness and weakness. Why does God turn somebodies, those who, according to ordinary standards, are generally recognized to be somebodies, into nobodies? "So that no one might boast in the presence of God" (1 Cor. 1:29). "No one" includes not just those who are deemed superior and seek to maintain their superiority but also those who are inferior but aspire to achieve superiority. God's action undercuts what Louise Schottroff has called the "structure of bragging" that motivates striving for superiority at whatever point in the social hierarchy one may be.[6]

God elevates the inferior and brings down the superior (for instance, by breaking the bows of the mighty and girding the feeble with strength, 1 Sam. 2:4). The God of the Hebrew Bible and of the Gospels does that. But if God did only that, we might be tempted

125

to think that God is the God of the resentful, as Nietzsche argued.[7] But God does *more* than that! (*Not* less than that!) God changes the standards according to which the inferiority/superiority scale is set, making, for instance and most notably, the crucified Christ, rather than the Roman emperor, "the Lord of glory" (1 Cor. 2:8). The God of the Hebrew Bible and of the Gospels does that too. But if God did only that ("only" might not be the right word), God would be the God of consistent meritocratic moralists who have made the downward movement of love the highest value and the basis of assessing who is up and who is down on the superiority scale. But God does *more* than that too, Paul insists! In getting rid of the practice of boasting, God cancels the standards of the kind of aspiration and striving that aim at superiority, *however* one construes what makes people superior. The goal isn't just for the tables, as they are set, to be turned: to make the strong weak and the weak strong, leaving the structure of bragging intact. The goal isn't even just to have the tables set entirely differently: to redefine what it means to be strong so that one strives for the right kind of superiority. *The goal is to have tables that do not need turning or resetting for each member of the social body to have equal honor and receive the same care*—as Paul goes on to argue in 1 Corinthians 12:15–26 (see chap. 4).

*This* is what you bought into, Paul says to the Corinthians in 1 Corinthians 1:26–31, when you responded to the call of God and when Jesus Christ, the true wisdom ("righteousness and sanctification and redemption," 1:30)[8] came to live in you and you in him. *All* boasting is excluded—except for boasting in the Lord: "Let the one who boasts, boast in the Lord," writes Paul, concluding the argument (1:31). He is quoting the prophet Jeremiah (9:24). The phrase "in the Lord" in Paul's quote is absent from the text of Jeremiah, who instead advises boasting in the "understanding and knowledge" of God. Paul inserts "in the Lord" to make *Jesus Christ* himself, not human attitude toward him, the object of boasting. Jesus Christ, the crucified Lord of glory, the source of true wisdom, power, and standing, is the end of boasting, the end of all superiority claims, and therefore the end of all striving for superiority. The new self, constituted by the indwelling Christ, boasts in Christ and makes no claims about being better than anyone else. Instead, like the crucified Christ, the new self shows its wisdom, power, and nobility by entering into solidarity with the foolish, weak, and despised, to honor them and care for them more than it honors and cares for itself.

## 2

In 1 Corinthians 1:26–31, as in Romans 3 and 4, Paul argues against striving for superiority based on how God saves humanity in Jesus Christ. In 1 Corinthians 4:6–7, he delegitimizes boasting based on how God works in creating, pulling away the final plank on which a boasting self could stand.

The argument is terse but powerful, and it consists of three rhetorical questions directed pointedly to each member of the opposing party (the "you" in the questions is in the second person singular): "Who makes you different from another? What do you have that you did not receive? And if you received it, why do you boast as if you did not receive?" (4:7).[9] The Corinthians' boasting implies that each would answer the first question—"What makes you something special?"—in roughly the following way: "I do. *I myself* make myself distinguished by my ability to discern true greatness, by choosing to associate with the winning leader, and therefore by my ability to lay the foundation to achieve wealth, might, and reputation that will come my way. All this I do with God's help. But God helps those who don't sit on their hands but strive to help themselves, which is what I am doing. Therefore, *I* merit any status I have in the present or might have in the future!"

Paul's second question, the core of his argument, implies some such response of the Corinthians to his first question. He formulates the second question to negate that implied response. "What do you have that you did not receive?" The expected—or at least appropriate—response is "Nothing!" Earlier, he argued that each received their righteousness from God. None of it is self-generated; all of it is Christ's righteousness. It belongs to each person by virtue of Christ living in them and being their righteousness. It is theirs as a gift and as "alien." Now he nudges them to affirm that the entirety of what each is—they themselves and everything ascribed to them and acquired by them—is also a gift. It is theirs by virtue of God's creative relating to them. Everything they are and everything they have is received. It is theirs only *as* received.

The "only" in the previous sentence may be misleading. Paul's claim that the self is "nothing" does not at all imply a complete erasure of the self and its replacement with God or Christ. Being nothing refers to a fleshly form of the self that is living in a world whose own "form . . . is passing away" (1 Cor. 7:31). It is a fragile and transitory self, threatened and anxious about its own being and standing. The new form of the self is constituted, elevated, and secured through the life of the resurrected Christ being lived in it and manifested through it. Even at its weakest—in a sense, *especially* at its weakest—*that* self is unconquerable.[10] Just a few verses before his second rhetorical question in 4:7, Paul puts the paradox between "having nothing" to boast in and "having everything" this way: "So let no one boast about people. For all things are yours" (3:21). What are the "all things" that belong to them and that make striving for superiority superfluous? Literally all things: "whether Paul or Apollos or Cephas or the world or life or death or the present or the future—all are yours"! And why? Because "you are Christ's, and Christ is God's" (3:22–23). This amazingly rich self is the *same self* that is nothing apart from what it has received! Being given Christ, each new self is given the entire world; they are a new creation, and they have the new creation— even if, at present, in weakness and suffering.

Paul reveals the consequence for boasting in the final rhetorical question, which assumes that the Corinthians agree with him that they have received everything they have. "If then you received it, why do you boast as if it were not a gift?" (1 Cor. 4:7 RSV). If you received everything as a gift, and if your existence as the recipient is also a gift, all ground for boasting is gone. Correspondingly, striving for superiority over others, seeking to make yourself better than others and glorying in that achievement, is possible only as an existential falsity. Striving for superiority, like boasting, rests on a lie. It is not just a lie that strivers and boasters tell themselves. More troublingly, that lie is part of the ideology that is the "wisdom" of the world that boasters have made their own.

A major challenge for Paul is to get the Corinthians to see that what organizes much of their lives—what generates the social distinctions in status under which they, "low and despised in the world," suffer and what keeps them quarreling in the church and taking sides with Apollos and against him (or with some imagined version of him against Apollos)—is, in fact, a lie. In the case of the rivalry the Corinthians have imagined between himself and Apollos, Paul wastes no time showing how foolish such a conception is.

## 3

In rivalrous ardor for personal advancement (*zēlos*) and ensuing contentiousness (*eris*), different factions identified with Paul or Apollos and pitted them against each other (1 Cor. 3:3–4), but Paul does not let himself be drawn into the factions' respective strivings for superiority. Rejecting comparisons and rankings, he instead sketches the relation between Apollos and himself as a model of how Corinthians should relate to one another (cf. 4:6).

"Who then is Apollos? Who is Paul?" (1 Cor. 3:5),[11] he writes, preparing his readers for his deflation of the status and achievements of both Paul and Apollos—and of themselves. The answer?

Servants through whom you came to believe, as the Lord assigned to each. I planted, Apollos watered, but God gave the growth. So

129

neither the one who plants nor the one who waters is anything, but only God who gives the growth. The one who plants and the one who waters have one purpose, and each will receive wages according to their own labor. For we are God's coworkers, working together; you are God's field, God's building. (3:5–9)

So, who *are* Apollos and Paul? For my purposes, the fact that Paul describes himself and Apollos as "servants" is less important than his claim that the task each of them has is not self-chosen and the capacities to fulfill it are not simply their own.[12] Each works as the Lord had given to him—what do they have that is not received? The work of each is important, even indispensable, but in comparison to God's work, making the field sprout with life, its value is negligible. Neither of them is "anything"!

Apollos and Paul are, then, doing God's work, and God is working through them. And yet each is a kind of "nobody." Neither is beating his chest, boasting in his superiority or trying to elbow his way into preeminence over the other. This kind of humility makes it possible for them, two people with different gifts and callings, to work in the same field, with a common purpose, and as a team: Paul planting (starting the church) and Apollos watering (nurturing the church). They act in the way Paul describes members of a body (1 Cor 12:12–31), a Christian community, acting toward one another—giving equal honor and the same care to each other.

———※———

"Each will receive wages according to their own labor" (1 Cor. 3:8)—at the end of history, Paul insists, not in its course. At the end is when the quality of everyone's work "will become visible, for the day will disclose it" (3:13). God will assess their labor and give them their corresponding wages. There may be a tension between, on the one hand, fieldhands having received from God all their capacities and their very selves (4:7) and being nothing in comparison to God, who gives growth (3:7)—or, in the formulation

130

from Philippians, between God effecting (*energōn*) in them both to will and to work (*energein*) (2:13)—and, on the other hand, each receiving a reward tailored to their work. How does God's working in their willing and acting fit with the differential wages corresponding to how each of them works? The fact that they are each getting a reward according to their labor may appear to leave space for striving for superiority and boasting. Later in this letter, Paul does seem to boast in what he has received: "But by the grace of God I am what I am, and his grace toward me has not been in vain. On the contrary, I worked harder than any of them" (1 Cor. 15:10). However, then he immediately weakens the claim to superiority over others, thereby canceling the boast, by bracketing it with an emphasis on God's agency in both making him who he is and enabling him to do what he has done: "I worked harder than any of them, though it was not I but the grace of God that is with me."

Perhaps we can come closer to resolving the tension in Paul between the "gift" of working and the "reward" for having worked if we relocate the reward. Ordinarily, we think of the reward at the day of judgment by analogy to the payment for work done, something laborers get for themselves—say, a crown to wear whose value corresponds to the effort and the quality of their moral or ministerial achievements, as sometimes in popular imagination. But that's not how Paul thinks of it. "For what is our hope or joy or crown of boasting before our Lord Jesus at his coming? Is it not you? Yes, you are our glory and joy!" (1 Thess. 2:19–20). People who embrace the way of Christ are, then, not the *work* for which Paul receives the reward; they cannot be, because it is God who gives life and growth in the field, while Paul, the laborer in the field, is "nothing." Instead, people, their growth in the superior knowledge of Christ, are the *reward*. Moreover, the reward—the boast in the Lord—is mutual: on the day of the Lord "we are your boast even as you are our boast" (2 Cor. 1:14). All those who attain to the resurrection of the dead are each other's joy, crown, and glory, and all together, we might add with Julian of Norwich, they are Christ's crown[13]—and in this they are also each other's reward. With such a reward in view, striving for superiority is oxymoronic.[14]

=== ‖ ===

Paul restricts the space for boasting not only by limiting it to boasting in the Lord but also by the way he thinks about the assessment of human beings and their work. Every act of boasting, whether in one's own work and standing or in that of another, presumes an *assessment*—as does, of course, every act of self-abnegation or denigration of others. As I noted earlier, it is important to Paul that self-assessments be truthful, made with "sober judgment" (Rom. 12:3). In 1 Corinthians 4, he expresses serious doubt over whether people are, in fact, capable of making truthful judgments about themselves and others:

> But with me it is a very small thing that I should be judged by you or by any human court. I do not even judge myself. I am not aware of anything against myself, but I am not thereby acquitted. It is the Lord who judges me. Therefore do not pronounce judgment before the time, before the Lord comes, who will bring to light the things now hidden in darkness and will disclose the purposes of the heart. Then each one will receive commendation from God. (vv. 3–5)

The Corinthians' assessment of Paul matters little to him, in part because he is a servant of Christ and a steward of God's mysteries. He is working for God and in God's "field" or "building" (1 Cor. 3:9, 16–17). What matters most is that he is faithful to *God*. That's one reason why the Corinthians' opinion of him matters little. The other is that they—and humans more generally—lack the ability to make correct judgments about others. The Corinthians don't have adequate knowledge about Paul's and Apollos's comparative achievements to assess whether Paul is inferior or superior to Apollos. Human beings are essentially opaque to one another. Their interior lives are mutually inaccessible. Their motivations and purposes, which in part make them who they are, are, as Paul writes, "hidden in darkness." That's why the ultimate assessment belongs to an all-seeing God, not to the Corinthians or to "any human court," a point Milton makes as well (chap. 3).

Perhaps surprisingly, the human courts that cannot be trusted are not only judgments that people make of others but also judgments people make of themselves. Paul's conscience is clear, he writes, but that does not put him in the clear; he cannot from that conclude that he is "justified" as God's steward. He is not sufficiently legible even to himself to make such a judgment; his own self is in darkness, and what he sees of it may be only what the self is willing to disclose. In a poem titled "Who Am I?" written during his imprisonment, Dietrich Bonhoeffer makes the same point powerfully. He reports both what his fellow prison inmates say about him and what he, more intimately, knows of himself. Then he continues,

> Who am I? This one or the other?
> Am I this one today and tomorrow another?
> Am I both at once? Before others a hypocrite
> And in my own eyes a pitiful, whimpering weakling?
> Or is what remains in me like a defeated army,
> Fleeing in disarray from victory already won?
> Who am I? They mock me, these lonely questions of mine.
> Whoever I am, thou knowest me; O God, I am thine![15]

Bonhoeffer might have learned from Paul his reticence to trust his assessment of himself. Paul does not judge himself either: he acts in the light he has and awaits the day for the final assessment of himself and his work. As he noted earlier, though, on account of Christ's righteousness, which became his when he entrusted himself to Christ (1 Cor. 1:30), he will be found justified even if all his work as a steward is proven faulty (3:13–15).

If any human court is inadequate, if neither others nor I can adequately assess me, how can I justify striving or claiming to be better than they are? How can I assume a position from which I can legitimately boast? My striving for superiority and my boasting are blind. I must wait for the day when the light will shine in dark spaces. And when it comes, I, along with everyone else, will receive praise—or censure—from God. Before that day, self-praise or self-disparagement and extolling or belittling others are all misplaced. Assessments of people are to be done in both provisional and noncompetitive ways. Boasting in one's superiority is excluded.

## 4

When the conflict with the Corinthians becomes fierce, Paul himself turns to boasting—even though, in his earlier polemic with them, he insists, on many grounds, that boasting is wrong! His first letter to the Corinthians did not resolve the tensions between them over attitudes toward power and status. What he wrote did not persuade them. His subsequent visit did not help either. As the end of 2 Corinthians, written a year or so after 1 Corinthians, attests, the tension between them was stronger than ever.[16] Now it is no longer Apollos whom the Corinthians are pitting against Paul but some other, unspecified leaders, whom Paul labels "super-apostles" (2 Cor. 11:15).

Chapters 10 to 12 contain Paul's self-defense and takedown of these super-apostles and, more importantly in his mind, a defense of the gospel of the crucified Christ he preached. Most of that text, however, turns out to be *one very long boast*! The Corinthians favor leaders who, with much more polished rhetoric than Paul's, proclaim the kind of theology of glory that Paul considers a betrayal of the gospel. The Corinthians still deem Paul and his theology of the cross to be inferior—which leads them to see as inferior the people who follow him. Contrary to what he argued in 1 Corinthians 1–4 and to his long-standing position, Paul boasts.

The Corinthians, he writes, have "forced" him to (cf. 2 Cor. 11:30; 12:1, 11). It could be that Paul is simply inconsistent: he is unable to act in all circumstances in accordance with what he thinks is one of the key characteristics of followers of Christ—namely, that they do not strive after or insist on their own superiority. He would then be like Milton, asserting his own superiority in the act of offering a brilliant poetic critique of superiority (see chap. 4). However, I will make the case that Paul remained consistent: that he is actually not boasting in this sense, though he comes very close to it.

Though Paul boasts with bitter abandon, he does so *in the character of a fool*. When he embraced Christ, he gave up on the *cursus honorum* and, by entrusting his life to Christ, affirmed the value of loving others more than himself and treating them as if they were "higher" than himself. That is the bedrock of his moral instruction, as I noted (chap. 4). But the Corinthians did not have eyes to see and hearts to embrace that new standard of value that was so contrary to the *cursus honorum*. In his first letter, Paul had explained what it takes to make the shift in the standard of values (1 Cor. 2)—the topic to which I will turn shortly (sec. 5)—to no avail. Hence, at the end of his second letter, he makes a desperate attempt to shake sense into them by assuming, for a moment, their value system (the "fleshly" standards of the present form of the world, 2 Cor. 11:18) and engaging in comparisons by portraying himself as equal and, in most important matters, superior to the super-apostles. The endeavor is intentionally foolish, he says plainly and more than once, but for him this is not "foolishness" as a state of feigned mental disturbance. It is, instead, a state of thinking, feeling, and relating to others according to the standards of the foolish and perishing world (1 Cor. 1:18) rather than "according to the Lord" (2 Cor. 11). Engaging in such "boastful undertaking" (11:17)—literally, being in a "state of boasting" (*hypostasei tēs kauchēseōs*)—*is* such foolishness.

As I read 2 Corinthians 10–12, Paul is gradually descending rhetorically into this "state of boasting," starting with "I wish you would put up with me in a little foolishness" (11:1) and bottoming out when he writes, "Are they [the super-apostles] ministers of Christ? I am talking like a madman—I am a better one" (11:23). Even earlier in 10:8, when he writes, "Now, even if I boast a little too much of our authority . . . I will not be ashamed of it," we can sense his unease about what he is about to do; he is preparing his readers for the folly to come. (He would have given in to their position had he claimed that boasting is just fine, perhaps a small transgression against good manners, as long as there isn't too much of it!)[17] Significantly, in 10:8–18 he is *not* comparing himself with others; he is measuring himself "by himself," which is, as Bultmann puts it, "comparison by achievement of the divinely given task."[18]

<hr />

When Paul fully takes on the role of the fool, in the so-called fool's speech (2 Cor. 11:16–12:10), he boasts *both* in the kinds of things in which the super-apostles boast and in which the Corinthians cheer them on (in his "strengths," like pedigree [11:22] or knowledge [11:6] or revelations [12:1–8]) *and* in the kinds of things in which the super-apostles would never boast and for which both the Corinthians and the super-apostles consider him to be an inferior apostle (in his "weaknesses," like persecutions and perils on mission assignments, 11:23–33). Now, one might think that, from Paul's perspective, the first kind of boasting would be bad because it is "according to human standards" but the second kind would be good: that this second kind would be boasting "with the Lord's authority" or, literally, "according to the Lord" (*kata kyrion*) (11:17). If this were the case, he would have been foolish when he engaged in the first kind of boasting but wise when he engaged in the second. But that would be a wrong reading of the text. Paul's most emphatic statement that his boasting is madness concerns his claim *that he is a better minister of Christ than the super-apostles*, a boast that is then immediately followed by a long

136

. supporting list of his sufferings, all of which highlight his weakness (11:23–33). It is not just that boasting in wrong things (strength) is acting "according to human standards"; *boasting of any kind,* even boasting in the most admirable achievements of sacrifice in humble service, is acting according to human standards. Even the "upside-down boast," to use N. T. Wright's phrase,[19] is a fleshly boast, a celebration of one's own achieved superiority over others.[20]

In 2 Corinthians 11:23–33, Paul describes himself as imitating the descent of Christ into the ignominy of service and crucifixion as portrayed in Philippians 2.[21] His point in Philippians 3 and 1 Corinthians 1–4 is that if he were to boast in his imitation of Christ, he would be boasting in himself and not in the Lord (see 1 Cor. 1:30; 2 Cor. 10:17). As he sees it, he is willing and able to undergo the sufferings in service to others because the resurrected Christ lives in him, because God enables him "both to will and to work for his good pleasure" (Phil. 2:13). In his account of the agency of a Christian, the "I" as a sovereign agent of the self's deeds no longer lives; Christ lives in the self, and the self lives by faith in Christ (Gal. 2:20; Phil. 3:3; 1 Cor. 1:31).[22] The boast therefore belongs to God and Christ, not to Paul. That's why boasting even in the context of the theology of the cross is problematic, and not just boasting in the context of the theology of glory. *Any* boasting or striving to be better than others is excluded, because all such boasting and striving must rely on the self's achievements and possessions to establish superiority and motivate others to recognize it. To strive for superiority and boast about it is to be a fool "according to the Lord."

By boasting, Paul displays the wrongness of boasting. Even if every word of one's own boasting is true, that very truth is existentially and morally tainted if it becomes an instrument in striving for or asserting one's superiority. It is possible for the content of one's claims about oneself to be true but for the pragmatics of those truth claims to be all wrong because they follow the standards of this perishing world (see 2 Cor. 12:6).

## 5

Paul frames both his critique of striving for superiority and his alternative to it in apocalyptic terms. One form of the world is passing away, its rulers coming to nothing (1 Cor. 2:6); another form of the world, the new creation marked by unconditional mutual honoring and care, is breaking out within it, like the first signs of spring, in the crucified and resurrected Jesus Christ and in the communities gathered around him. The shifting and still permeable line demarcating the two forms of the world runs not only between the outside (the "world") and these communities (the "church") but also within these communities—in fact, within each of its members. The communities have not yet been fully saved but "are being saved"; the world has not yet perished but "is perishing" (1:18). That deeper, complex reality of the church and the world with the crucified and resurrected Christ in the middle of it is the mystery, not visible to the world, that God has revealed (2:7).

On the surface, church communities were marginal, often persecuted minorities, even though the resurrection life and powers of the new form of the world were at work within them. On the surface, the wider world, or at least some portion of it, was rising from strength to strength, even though it was afflicted by terminal illness. The center of the empire, Rome, had expanded its reach, establishing colonies; the riches were growing, knowledge was increasing, *ludi publici* (public games) and more intimate pleasures were being enjoyed, and races for honors were being won—and mostly lost, of course. The elevation of some meant the disempowerment, immiseration, exploitation, and degradation of many. That was not a bug in the system but a feature; let the poor elevate themselves, for if they are helped, the order and stability—and dynamism in today's order marked by acceleration—of the whole system will be compromised. Striving for superiority was at the heart of the wisdom, and power, and glory of that form of the world, and not just of those at the very top but of all those who were aspiring to be at the top, or at least to ascend above others; having internalized the system, they ran their own smaller, but for them no less important, honor races. As most of us do today.

Paul saw this striving and seemingly thriving world as perishing. His point was not just that it was bound to be destroyed by someone greater—a stronger invader—and eventually by the judgment of God at the end of the ages. (One such vision of both the character of Rome and its demise in the fires of divine judgment is found in Revelation 17:1–19:10.)[23] His point was also that this world was sick and dying, notwithstanding its rosy cheeks and bulging muscles, growing knowledge and polished speeches, decadent attire and sumptuous meals. By striving for superiority, some were undermining and, at times, destroying others, and all were destroying themselves. What looked like a logic of increase in life's power was a logic of self-destruction obscured by the shimmering of achieved and aspired fake glory. In the figure of Satan, Milton describes one version of the drive to self-elevation and of the havoc it wreaks upon the world and, ultimately, upon strivers for superiority themselves, plunging them into the abyss (see chap. 3).

As we have seen, Paul contrasts the way of Christ with striving for honor. One is life "according to the Lord," and the other is life "according to flesh." Instead of holding onto the privileges of being the highest, Christ descended to become a servant even of the most despised humans. Instead of taking honor from others and amassing it for himself, he sought to elevate all into the glory in which all goods and all honors are shared. This is the logic of the enhancement of power and life, but for *all* rather than for oneself; there is no comparative superiority here, only the generous dispersal of conditions for excellence. In his entire earthly life of service, Jesus Christ was the "Lord of glory," a point Paul states tersely in 1 Corinthians 2:8 but on which he elaborates in Philippians 2:6–11. The rulers of the present form of the world—the guardians of its way of life and of the poisoned fruit it grows in abundance—could not recognize this. That's why they crucified him. Dying in the greatest shame outside the gate of Jerusalem, he was no less glorious than when sitting at the right hand of Glory.

====

Even as followers of Christ, the Corinthians had a hard time recognizing the *crucified* Christ as the Lord of glory. It is one thing to see God in the resurrection; it is much more challenging to embrace the redefined glory shining in the foolishness of the cross. How does one make Jesus Christ and his way, as Paul sketches it, acceptable and accepted? Paul struggles to persuade the Corinthians with all the means at his disposal (minus polished rhetoric, which would undermine the point he is making)—and fails. To the Corinthians, as to the rulers of the world whose form is perishing, the theology of the cross is a theology of weakness and defeat. The Corinthians are looking for leaders who will rescue them from living close to the bottom of the social hierarchy and elevate them to positions of greater power and honor. They are even willing to endure abuse from those leaders, suffer their heavy-handed authoritarianism (2 Cor. 11:20), just to take a few steps up the hierarchy—and have a few more people below them. Paul is not convincing. But why?

What wisdom is to Paul is foolishness to the Corinthians, and vice versa. The difference between them is not so much values (though that is the case too) as it is *alternative standards of evaluation*: "according to the flesh" versus "according to the Lord." Such standards of evaluation—"tables of value" (Friedrich Nietzsche), "rules of preference" (Max Scheler), or "hypergoods" (Charles Taylor)[24]—provide the criteria by which we assign value or disvalue. Between these standards, the gap is nearly unbridgeable. In Plato's dialogue *Crito*, Socrates discusses with Crito a view they both share: "One should never do wrong in return [for having been wronged], nor do any man harm, no matter what he may have done to you." What happens if people disagree about this principle? Socrates responds, "There is no common ground between those who hold this view and those who do not, but they inevitably despise each other's views."[25] "Despising" may be too strong a reaction to a person espousing unacceptable "tables of value," but Socrates's point is otherwise unimpeachable. Applied to our topic, there seems to be little common ground between the meta-values of the ascending race of honors and those of status-indifferent service to others, between striving for superiority and striving to be excellent at treating others as if they were higher than oneself.

Commitment to Jesus Christ and the presence of the Spirit are the common ground between Paul and the Corinthians. But how does one determine what it means for Jesus Christ to be "wisdom" (1 Cor. 1:30)? One mounts arguments in favor of one interpretation or another, which is what Paul does. He is convinced, though, that one will know the meaning of God's wisdom only when one gives up thinking and living "according to the flesh" and begins aspiring to think and live "according to the Lord." That shift itself, Paul believes, is not—perhaps *cannot* be—a result of reasoning on its own. He himself did not embrace Jesus Christ, his wisdom and his *cursus pudorum*, simply as a result of study and deep reflection. Jesus appeared to Paul to reveal to him the "gospel," Paul's summary word for Christ himself and his way of life (Gal. 1:11–12; 1 Cor. 2:13). Hence, he points the Corinthians to revelation as well. God's wisdom is "secret and hidden," known to God alone and, in the present age, appearing under its seeming opposite. "Now we have received not the spirit of the world but the Spirit that is from God, so that we may understand the gifts bestowed on us by God" (1 Cor. 2:12). What the Spirit gives is Christ, the incarnate wisdom, and, with Christ, "the mind of Christ" (2:16). Put slightly differently, we need to encounter the prototype, as Kierkegaard called Christ, the embodiment of God's wisdom in the story of a concrete life, and we need eyes capable of recognizing him as such.

The appeal to revelation, to the presence of Christ and the Spirit removing the appearance of foolishness from God's wisdom, is ultimately an invitation to *trust*. The way of Christ, his and his followers' "descent" into service, cannot be intellectually and fully secured from without. Those who approach it without the Spirit and outside the "mind of Christ" will likely be "unable to understand" it (1 Cor. 2:14). The eyes of those who embrace Christ in the power of the Spirit will be opened, and they will recognize him as the crucified Lord of glory. In the same act, they will also discover themselves as the people whose glory and true excellence is to treat each other as if the other were more important than they are themselves. To such, another kind of glory, and a lasting one, is promised as well.

# 6

# From Jesus to Genesis:
# On Biblical Discomfort with
# Striving for Superiority

In the preceding chapters, I explored critiques of striving for
superiority and the alternative to it in three Christian thinkers:
starting with Kierkegaard, then going back in time to Milton,
and then to the apostle Paul, arguably the first Christian theologian. This may give the impression that Paul was the first in the
Christian tradition to identify striving for superiority as a major
problem. But that would be the wrong inference to draw. Though
Paul engages the problem in a more sustained way than any other
biblical writer, he was not the first in the biblical traditions to
critique striving for superiority. The concern goes back to Jesus
(as portrayed in the Gospels) and all the way to accounts of the
election of Israel and the call of Abraham. Here, at the end of my
exploration, it is important to give honor where honor is due and
briefly sketch this longer history.

All three of my interlocutors are aware of this history and build
on elements of it. Though Kierkegaard was deeply influenced by

Paul, he largely expounds his critique of superiority by drawing on the Gospels, notably in his expositions of the Sermon on the Mount and the parable of the Pharisee and the tax collector (Luke 18:9–14). As for Milton, Paul's hymn to Christ in Philippians 2 frames both of his great poems, *Paradise Lost* and *Paradise Regained*, and he sketches the alternative to striving for superiority by building on Jesus's temptations in the wilderness. Though Paul does not refer to the teaching of Jesus in engaging the problem of striving for superiority—he seems not to have known the teachings of Jesus as recorded in the Gospels—he grounds it in the death and resurrection of Christ and makes much of the example of Abraham. In this final chapter I aim to root the preceding discussion in these seminal texts without attempting to offer a full treatment of the topic as it appears in the Gospels and Hebrew Bible. I end by bringing to surface one of the submerged red threads of this book as a whole: the relation of striving for superiority to God's providence.

## 1

The strongest case Jesus makes against striving for superiority is in response to the two disciples who request positions of eminence at his right and left hands when he is installed as the messianic ruler of the coming kingdom:

> James and John, the sons of Zebedee, came forward to him and said to him, "Teacher, we want you to do for us whatever we ask of you." And he said to them, "What is it you want me to do for you?" And they said to him, "Appoint us to sit, one at your right hand and one at your left, in your glory." But Jesus said to them, "You do not know what you are asking. Are you able to drink the cup that I drink or be baptized with the baptism that I am baptized with?" They replied, "We are able." Then Jesus said to them, "The cup that I drink you will drink, and with the baptism with which I am baptized you will be baptized, but to sit at my right hand or

at my left is not mine to appoint, but it is for those for whom it has been prepared."

When the ten heard this, they began to be angry with James and John. So Jesus called them and said to them, "You know that among the gentiles those whom they recognize as their rulers lord it over them, and their great ones are tyrants over them. But it is not so among you; instead, whoever wishes to become great among you must be your servant, and whoever wishes to be first among you must be slave of all. For the Son of Man came not to be served but to serve and to give his life a ransom for many." (Mark 10:35–45)

From one angle, this passage contrasts ruling and serving. James and John want to rule, and Jesus tells them that a key part of his mission is to establish an alternative social order in which those with power and wealth do not rule over the weak and the poor but all serve each other. He has not come to "lord it over" others. In a parallel passage in Luke 22:24–27, Jesus implies that he does not want to be called "benefactor" either—an aspiration of many rulers, aristocrats, and officials in the Roman Empire who use gift-giving "to secure the loyalty of those over whom they rule."[1] Instead, he has come to serve, even to the point of death. Proper rulers serve. They neither impose rule by violence nor pay for loyalty with gifts. Jesus had already given them that very lesson, with emphasis (Mark 9:35). James and John are on board with this, though without fully understanding to what they are consenting—perhaps in part because the dazzle of Jesus's glory that they had witnessed on the mountain of transfiguration and in which they hoped to share was clouding their judgment (9:2–3). They, too, heard the voice declare Jesus as "my Son, the Beloved" (9:7) and thereby signify not just how uniquely God loved him but also that, like Abraham's and Jacob's beloved sons, he will undergo a great suffering.[2] In making their request, James and John imply that they understand all this—they are willing to drink the cup of service and be baptized by the baptism of sacrificial death, as Jesus will be.

But James and John are not merely aspiring to rule with Jesus. In requesting of Jesus to appoint them "to sit, one at your right hand and one at your left, in your glory" (Mark 10:37), they are jockeying for status—higher than anyone but Jesus. They imagine themselves as the two arms of the uncontestable supreme head of the kingdom of glory. The anger of the other ten disciples when they find out about the request is part of the ongoing struggle for superiority among the disciples, a powerful drive with deep roots in the human condition, as we have seen throughout this book. In the previous chapter in Mark, we find them all arguing "with one another who was the greatest" (9:34). Jesus led only three disciples up with him to witness his transfiguration—Peter and the two aspirants for the highest status (9:2–8). The remainder stayed, and instead of getting to see Jesus transfigured, listen to Elijah and Moses speak with Jesus, and hear the divine voice speak, they experience the shame of Jesus's reprimand for failure to cast a demon out of an afflicted boy (9:14–29). The ensuing quarrel about who is the greatest seems almost preprogrammed: the pride of the smaller, seemingly favored group clashes with the humiliation of the rest. In response, Jesus sits down, calls them to himself, and from the position of authority, gives them the rule: "Whoever wants to be first must be last of all and servant of all" (9:35).

We can assume that James and John had heard and accepted the lesson and yet missed its main point—habits as old as humanity itself do not die easily. They go behind the backs of the other disciples and, instead of making a request, issue a rather brazen demand to Jesus: "Teacher, we want you to do for us whatever we ask of you" (10:35). Clandestinely, they push themselves ahead and, in effect, demand preferential treatment. They aren't surprised by Jesus's initial response; they assume he is simply checking whether they are ready to pay the cost, to suffer as Jesus will—to be the last, the servants, the slaves. They are aligned with what they take to be Jesus's stated qualifications for rule, for being "first." But how many "firsts" can there be? Exactly two, they seem to

146

reason, one on each of Jesus's sides (even if it is true that the one on the right will be just a bit higher than the one on the left, for the place on the right was deemed to be higher [cf. 1 Peter 3:22]). The great sacrifice, they think, will be the payment for the privilege of unmatched superiority. But by itself this will not do, for others may make equal sacrifice. Jesus's preferential treatment would be needed to secure these positions. Hence their request. The other ten disciples are angry—likely because the request of the two, if granted, would rob them of a chance to get the same reward. On this reading, all the disciples seem to act like the "benefactors" who Jesus censured, only with different conditions for acquiring and keeping status (see discussion on "upside-down boast" in chap. 5, sec. 4). Instead of beneficence that merely lessens wealth, the condition they accept is self-sacrificial service. Still, each is looking to secure his own superiority.

—— ‡‡‡ ——

In the second part of his answer to James and John, Jesus undercuts such reasoning. Their destiny, he tells them, will indeed be like his, marked by great suffering in service of others. But that will not qualify them for the highest positions: "But to sit at my right hand or at my left is not mine to appoint, but it is for those for whom it has been prepared" (Mark 10:40). The only other place where Mark mentions positions on the right and left of Jesus are in the crucifixion scene, with two men crucified on either side of him. Was Mark implying that the crucifixion—drinking the cup that Jesus drank and being baptized with his baptism—*is* the glory?[3] Even if we don't choose this option, Jesus's main point is clear: status in the world to come is *not earned* through sacrificial service.

There are several problems with the idea of earning rule and status with service. First, if arduous service to all is what merits status—note, though, that James and John could not simply rely on the workings of the meritocratic principle to secure them the highest positions—then it seems that the same principle should apply in the life to come. Some kind of merit would be required to keep the status, for merit was needed to acquire it. It is possible to think of the world to come as a perfect meritocracy, but if that were so, it would be hard to imagine it as a world of love. It is better to assume that in the kingdom of glory no arduous service attending to the needs of others will be necessary, let alone sacrificing one's life for others. Service there will be nothing other than the joy of love, the activity of lovingly enhancing one another's joy.[4] But how could such activity *earn* one's status?

Second, earning the two highest honors is problematic because every single disciple of Jesus is called to emulate Jesus and serve others sacrificially; they all are to serve one another.[5] How many firsts are there in the world to come? *All* those who serve *all*—which might be saying that God alone is the first, and all denizens of the world to come are equally second. The two highest positions, one on the left and the other on the right of the reigning Jesus, do not exist. (In his response to John and James, Jesus might be assuming that they do exist for the sake of argument, which deconstructs the whole idea.) James and John—or whomever they got the idea from—might have invented the two positions, and the invention was the product of striving for superiority.

The only passage in the New Testament where we get a sense of who will sit next to the reigning Jesus is in the book of Revelation. Speaking to the church in Laodicea, the ascended Jesus says, "To the one who conquers I will give a place with me on my throne, just as I myself conquered and sat down with my Father on his throne" (Rev. 3:21). Who will conquer? Not just one or two but *all* those who enter into glory. If we use Revelation to solve the puzzle of God's appointment to positions of honor in the world to come, James and John's clandestine operation to secure the highest position for themselves gets exposed as completely misdirected striving. No disciple will have a position higher than any other; all will sit on the same throne.[6]

148

(An alternative view is that there will be differential standings and that these will be assigned on the basis of some achievement—for instance, leading others to righteousness [Dan. 12:3]. In this case, *relative* standing will be morally irrelevant; it will matter only how close to the moral ideal one is, not how one stacks up against others. Aiming at this mere relative standing would, if we assumed this reading, be an unworthy goal of James and John's striving.)

Third, in Mark 10, the paradigmatic example of service is Jesus. Given who he is, he cannot *gain* in status by serving and dying on behalf of others. The title he uses of himself in the passage is the "Son of Man." It likely harkens back to "the one like a son of man" in Daniel 7 (ESV), who is an exalted figure with everlasting dominion over "all peoples, nations, and languages" (Dan. 7:14). In Mark, Jesus does not receive this status, as in Daniel; he comes with it. He serves and gives his life as the one with exalted status. This corresponds to what we find in Mark 9, where the voice from heaven declares Jesus to be God's Son, marking him for suffering (9:7). Jesus does not become the Son of Man or the Son of God, does not increase his status, on account of his service and his death on the cross.[7] The lesson for the disciples is that service is not a means for elevation above others. Service is a means to alleviate suffering or increase joy of those served. For those who serve, it is not a means but the goal in itself. Service is not a means to glory but the content of glory (though not its only form).

On my reading, with the statement "Whoever wants to be first must be last of all and servant of all" (Mark 9:35), Jesus is not turning striving for superiority on its head, as if to say that inferiority is the new superiority. If he were, he would not have ended the disciples' argument about who among them was the greatest; he would have encouraged the argument to continue on different terms—those of the meritocratic moralists we encountered earlier. Each one would now simply strive to somehow be *more* the servant of all than the others! As I read the passage, Jesus is saying that being superior to someone else is a nonvalue. It is wrong to make superiority one's goal and argue about who is the greatest. Striving to be superior to someone else is a vice.

**2**

The critique of striving for superiority does not begin with Jesus. We can find it in many places in the Hebrew Bible. Qohelet, for instance, takes up the issue (see chap. 1). Though striving for superiority stimulates effort and improves skill, it is nonetheless doomed to futility. In the preface, I commented briefly on the story of Cain and Abel in Genesis, noting that, whatever else the story is about, it is in part a critique of striving for superiority. In this case, it leads to murder designed to reestablish the order of superiority that God's acceptance of Abel's offering had upended.[8] Milton argued that the fall in Gen. 3 was largely about striving for superiority, though he could be accused of projecting into the story convictions drawn mainly from the New Testament.

If only these few passages from the Hebrew Bible were concerned with striving for superiority, we might rightly conclude that the theme is marginal and that the Hebrew Bible differs from the New Testament in this regard. After all, both Jesus's and Paul's critiques of striving for superiority are derived from the very purpose of Jesus's mission: he came to serve, and his kind of service defines not just excellence but also true glory (see chap. 4). But to draw such a contrast in judgment about striving for superiority between the Hebrew Bible and the New Testament—marginal in former, central in the latter—would be to miss the denunciation of striving for superiority contained in the founding events of Judaism: the call of Abraham and the election of Israel. Jon Levenson and, in his trail, Shai Held highlight the polemic against superiority implied in Abraham's call and Israel's election. I will largely follow their readings of Genesis and Deuteronomy as I explore the issue. My goal is to highlight aspects of a Jewish take on striving for superiority.

===꜒꜒꜒===

Consider first the call of Abraham, or rather Abram, as was his name before God renamed him. In Genesis 11, we read that Terah took his son Abram and his daughter-in-law Sarai and that "they went out together from Ur of the Chaldeans to go into the land of Canaan" (11:31). The group never reached Canaan and settled for a while in Haran. We know nothing about Abram—his moral or intellectual qualities or his doings and achievements or lack of them—before God addressed him after the death of his father:

> Go from your country and your kindred and your father's house to the land that I will show you. I will make of you a great nation, and I will bless you and make your name great, so that you will be a blessing. I will bless those who bless you, and the one who curses you I will curse, and in you all the families of the earth shall be blessed. (12:1–3)

Commenting on the call of Abram, Levenson writes,

> In the biblical narrative, the earliest sign that God would form a special relationship with the people of Israel occurs when, for the first time, he speaks to Abraham, the grandfather of Israel (or Jacob, to use his other name), promising him that he will be a great nation and a byword or source of blessing. But why Abraham? Genesis reports absolutely nothing to suggest that the future patriarch already merited such a distinction more than did, say, his brother Nahor.[9]

Singling Abram out for greatness from all humanity seems arbitrary.[10] Why Abram? Contrast Noah with Abraham. Noah was favored and saved from the flood because he alone "was a righteous man, blameless in his generation" (Gen. 6:9). Nothing like that is said of Abram; no exceptional qualities of his are mentioned, such as righteousness, religious zeal, or negotiating skills (visible later in bargaining with God about Sodom). Instead, Abram possesses a kind of negative quality, making it unlikely that the great promise that comes with the call could ever be fulfilled: Abram's wife, Sarai, "was barren" and "had no child" (11:30). Throughout history, starting with Genesis itself, diverse explanations for the call of Abram have been offered to remove the scandal of what seems like God's arbitrariness.[11] Those familiar with the Bible will know that this kind of arbitrariness of bestowed favor has a name: grace. Abram did not merit the call in any way; he was given a free gift of that call—and with the gift a responsibility, which arguably involves striving for excellence.

——— ❦ ———

To the grace of Abram's call in Genesis corresponds the "unreason" of Israel's election in Deuteronomy:

> For you are a people holy to the Lord your God; the Lord your God has chosen you out of all the peoples on earth to be his people, his treasured possession. It was not because you were more numerous than any other people that the Lord set his heart on you and chose you, for you were the fewest of all peoples. It was because the Lord loved you and kept the oath that he swore to your ancestors that the Lord has brought you out with a mighty hand and redeemed you from the house of slavery, from the hand of Pharaoh king of Egypt. (Deut. 7:6–8)

God singled out the people of Israel, among all the nations, to be God's treasured possession. Again, why? The text states that God did *not* "set his heart" on Israel because the people of Israel were more numerous than other people. The size of the population stands here for any positive quality that they may possess— religious receptivity, moral excellence, or high intelligence, for instance. No such qualities are part of the given reason. The sole reason for election is no proper reason at all: Israel is a treasured possession of God because the Lord "set his heart on you" (v. 7) and "loved you" (v. 8). God had simply fallen in love with Israel, Levenson writes, noting that "set his heart on you" is best translated here as "take a passion to." God's choice of the people of Israel "is being ascribed to an affair of the heart, as it were, and not to any attribute or accomplishment that they had to their credit at the time."[12] The reason for God's choice of Israel is the same as God's choice of Abraham, the difference in vocabulary notwithstanding: "The point Genesis makes implicitly Deuteronomy makes explicitly."[13] Deuteronomy 7:8 connects the two: because God loved Israel and was faithful to the promise to Abraham, God rescued the people of Israel from Egypt and constituted them into a nation.

God's bypassing of attributes and achievements in call and election, arbitrariness in singling out one person and choosing one people, has consequences for any claims to superiority. Taking up this issue explicitly, Levenson writes that the unmerited character of God's call and election

> is important because it makes it impossible for the attentive hearer of the text to identify chosenness with superiority—a mistake that is very common today, especially among those who find the whole idea of chosenness distasteful. For, like Abraham when God first speaks to him, Israel does not work its way into the role of the beneficiary of God's concern. As the text in Deuteronomy goes on to say, the very liberation of its hearers from the Egyptian house of bondage is not the result of anything the people did or even of the unmerited favor they have directly received from their divine redeemer: it results instead from the oath that God made to the patriarchs generations earlier (Deut. 7:8).

The descendants, then, have inherited their lofty status. They have not *achieved* it. It is a gift, not a reward. In response, they should feel not pride but gratitude, not satisfaction with their performance in the past but a profound challenge to live up to their divine benefactor's expectations in the future.[14]

The nature of the call to Abraham and the basis for the election of Israel allow for no claim to superiority and provide no basis for pride. Israel's status is not achieved but imparted—"ascribed," in the language of sociology.

⚎ ⵂ ⚎

Jewish scholars have traced the pushback against striving for superiority all the way back to the account of creation in Genesis 1. Before creating humans, God created aquatic, avian, and terrestrial animals, in that order, and in each of these categories God created animals "of every kind" (1:20–25). Nahum Sarna writes in his commentary on Genesis,

> It is noteworthy that the recurrent formula "of every kind," hitherto encountered with the emergence of every living thing, is here omitted. There is only one human species. The notion of all humankind deriving from one common ancestry directly leads to the recognition of the unity of the human race, notwithstanding the infinite diversity of human culture.[15]

The sages of the Mishna find pushback against striving for superiority in the account of the creation of Adam (and Eve). Why was Adam created alone? they ask. Here is one reason they give:

> And this was done due to the importance of maintaining peace among people, so that one person will not say to another: My father, i.e., progenitor, is greater than your father. And it was also so that the heretics who believe in multiple gods will not say: There are many authorities in Heaven, and each created a different person. And this serves to tell of the greatness of the Holy One, Blessed be He, as when a person stamps several coins with one seal, they are

all similar to each other. But the supreme King of kings, the Holy One, Blessed be He, stamped all people with the seal of Adam the first man, as all of them are his offspring, and not one of them is similar to another.[16]

The text makes two related claims about striving for superiority, versions of which we have already encountered in the course of our study. First, because asserting one's superiority and striving for superiority is inherently competitive, it undermines social peace. Second, even though each human being is unique, our common origin grounds equal dignity of all and undercuts any claim to superiority of one human being and of one people over others.[17]

## 3

Two of the most intense strivers for superiority in the Hebrew Bible are the grandson and great-grandson of Abraham—Jacob and his son Joseph. Both also undergo a transformation, turning at least partly away from near ruthless competitiveness. (New Testament strivers for superiority of comparable intensity are Jesus's disciples James and John, as well as Paul before his encounter with Christ.) In my brief exploration of Jacob's and Joseph's striving, I lean on Shai Held's *The Heart of Torah* and his Jewish interlocutors. In another book of his, *Judaism Is about Love*, Held's account of self-worth is sketched explicitly against the backdrop of striving for superiority. In contrast to self-boasting by comparison with others—"I might be worthless, but I'm smarter or better looking than they are"—"Jewish theology," Held writes, "insists that genuine self-worth is never competitive or comparative, never purchased at the expense of others."[18] In *The Heart of Torah*, in essays on Jacob and Joseph, Held does not explicitly explore striving for superiority, but I will bend his exploration in that direction. In the process, a theme that was present but submerged in my earlier treatments of striving for superiority will surface: the relation between striving for superiority and divine providence.

≡Ⅲ≡

Jacob's story is defined by striving for superiority over Esau, his older twin brother. The two struggled for superiority even in the womb of their mother (Gen. 25:22–26), and the conflicting preferences of their parents—Esau was Isaac's favorite, Jacob was Rebekah's—intensifies the struggle. Jacob is after Esau's two great "advantages": the status of the firstborn and the expected paternal blessing.

One day Esau returns from the field and, referring to Jacob's lentil stew, says, "Let me eat some of that red stuff, for I am famished!" (Gen. 25:30). Jacob responds with a hard bargain: "First sell me your birthright" (v. 31). Uncouth and in the grip of irresistible craving, Esau takes the offer. "He ate and drank and rose and went his way," we read, and what follows is a damning comment from the narrator: "Thus Esau despised his birthright" (v. 34). Esau might be a brute, but as we read the story, it is Jacob's character that worries us. How ruthlessly ambitious must a man be to demand from his brother such a high price for a single, simple meal? Held quotes a fifteenth-century rabbi, Isaac Abravanel: "Had Jacob been blameless and upright, how could he have dared to tell his older brother to sell him his birthright for . . . a contemptible price such as a bowl of lentil stew."[19]

Jacob shows himself even more morally callous in agreeing to Rebekah's plan to steal Esau's paternal blessing. As Esau is hunting for game to make a meal for his father and then receive the promised blessing, Rebekah cooks a similar meal to the one Isaac expects, and Jacob dons Esau's clothes and impersonates him as he brings the meal to his father. Deceived on account of his old age, Isaac blesses Jacob, thinking it is Esau. When Esau shows up shortly thereafter, both he and Isaac are devastated and condemn the shameless ruse. Esau's bitter cry is one of the most poignant in the entire Bible: "Have you only one blessing, father? Bless me, me also, father!" (27:38). The blessing he gets is far inferior to the one given to Jacob. Crucially, Jacob has achieved the superiority over Esau he sought: "Be lord over your brothers, and may your mother's sons bow down to you," Isaac has said in his blessing (27:29).

Commenting on both stories together, Held writes, "The Torah takes an extremely dim view of Jacob's trickery; he is made to pay for his deception the rest of his life."[20] Still, God loves Jacob; in fact, God seems to have ordained just that outcome. Despite this trickery, Jacob becomes the progenitor of the people of Israel. That sacred end, however, does not justify the evil of his unscrupulous struggle for superiority.

—※—

As Rebekah was partial to Jacob, so Jacob is partial to Joseph— the firstborn son of his favorite wife Rachel and a child of his old age. Jacob is a "doting father," and it is clear to the entire clan that Jacob loves Joseph "more than all his brothers" (Gen. 37:4). His older brothers are set against him; whoever among them manages the family business "stationed him with the sons of the slave woman (30:3–13), the lowest ranking siblings."[21]

Basking in his superiority and seeking to enhance it, the young narcissist makes one self-undermining step after another. First, while tending the flock with his older brothers, he brings "a bad report of them to their father" (37:2)—the Hebrew word for "bad" suggests it was not truthful but false and malicious. Second, Joseph smugly tells first his brothers and then his father two dreams in which they all "bow to the ground before" him (v. 10). Third, his father visibly singles him out by making him alone an ornamented robe (v. 3). The self-infatuated folly that costs Joseph his freedom was that he decided to wear it when his father sent him to see if all was well with his brothers and their flock near Shechem. Joel Kaminsky comments, "Like many a child who has been given a toy that his siblings have not received, [Joseph] is flaunting his favored status in front of his brothers for his own ego gratification."[22]

After his brothers sell him into slavery, he ends up in Egypt and, handsome and gifted as he is, works himself up to be an "overseer in his [master's] house and over all that he had" (Gen. 39:5). Both his Egyptian master and the narrator ascribe Joseph's success to God. Joseph himself "makes no mention of God at all," writes Held. "The reader is thus left to wonder whether Joseph 'assume[s] that] he attained this position on his own and that his charisma was for no greater purpose than to live a comfortable life.'"[23]

Unjustly imprisoned after the incident with Potiphar's wife—for which he nonetheless might bear a share of blame, as some rabbinic commentators argue[24]—he undergoes a transformation. In prison, where he becomes known as an interpreter of dreams, he deflects from himself, insisting that it is God, not he, who interprets dreams. He does the same when summoned before Pharaoh: "It is not I [who can tell the meaning of any dream]; God will give Pharaoh a favorable answer" (Gen. 41:16). He seems to recognize God as the source of his capacities and achievements. Years later, when he reveals himself to his brothers, who had come to buy food in Egypt to save Jacob's clan from starvation, he tells them that, though they did the abominable deed of selling him into slavery, "God sent me [here] before you to preserve life" (45:5). Instead of boosting himself, he now sees his talents and his journey to Egypt as God's gifts.

Yet he remains steadfast to the very end in his ruthless pursuit of ever greater power and wealth—under Pharaoh. When the great famine comes as God revealed through Joseph that it would, he does not share with afflicted people the food stored during the years of plenty. He sells it to them until he buys up all the land and all the people for Pharaoh (47:20–23). Administrative brilliance perhaps, but also a dismal failure to walk in God's ways.[25] Ultimately, Joseph used God's gifts to elevate himself to the highest rank available and to grow as powerful as he could without regard to the dire consequences for the great majority of the population.

Levenson sums up the great irony of Joseph's adult life: "Brought to Egypt as a slave, Joseph now becomes Egypt's enslaver." And not just Egypt's. When a new king arose over Egypt who did not know Joseph (Exod. 1:8), "the House of Israel found themselves once again on the wrong end of the enslavement process."[26] Joseph, we are told, prepared this eventual oppressive political system. His thirst for power and self-elevation paved the way for both the salvation and the enslavement of Jacob's descendants.

━━ ⅲ ━━

"Even though you intended to do harm to me, God intended it for good, in order to preserve a numerous people, as he is doing today" (50:20). These words of Joseph, addressed to his brothers near the end of Genesis, point to divine providence at work. This providence, informed by God's unconditional loyalty to the descendants of Jacob, is a hallmark of the entire book of Genesis, as Marilynne Robinson has portrayed so compellingly in *Reading Genesis*.[27] Just as God turned the cruelty of Joseph's brothers into the means of their salvation, so God is at work to lead individual destinies, family affairs, and world events to fulfill God's intention for all humanity. The same is true to a significant degree about the vice of striving for superiority we encounter so frequently in Genesis—Cain's attempt to reassert his position of superiority by killing his brother, the attempt of the builders' of the tower of Babel to reach the heavens, Sarah's efforts to preserve the primacy of her posterity over Hagar's, and Jacob's and Joseph's striving for primacy over their brothers. Human striving for superiority is folded into God's purposes.

We may be tempted to think that in Genesis God's providence plays the same function as that of an "invisible hand," according to Adam Smith, in modern economies: that it transforms private vices of selfishness, pride, and striving for superiority into public goods that fuel much of civilizational progress. Dostoevsky's Pyotr Petrovich of *Crime and Punishment* puts well popular simplifications of the idea: I acquire "solely and exclusively for myself" and

159

"I am thereby precisely acquiring for everyone."[28] This crass idea also illustrates an important and dubious transformation that the idea of an "invisible hand" has brought about: we no longer think of self-interest and striving for superiority as vices at all. To many, they have become virtues—or just what we humans do. This turning of erstwhile vices into virtues was aided by the evolutionary account of human origins, in which self-interest and the competition of individuals and groups are necessary drivers of development. Pursuing self-interest and competing is what we humans do—and when we collaborate in the process, we call the collaboration "altruism."[29]

In contrast, Genesis is unsparing in its account of the lives of the progenitors of the very people who produced the text and whose foundational stories it is telling. It resists the temptation to transmute their vices into virtues—or, for that matter, to hide them from sight. Yet it also insists that God's intentions were being achieved not only through imperfect and corrupt human beings but through their very moral failures. Genesis condemns Jacob for tricking Esau out of birthright and blessing *and* it sees God at work in his becoming the progenitor of the people of Israel—even with the help of his sinful schemes. It condemns Joseph for narcissistic striving for superiority throughout his life *and* it recognizes that the striving that it condemns was the means of Israel's salvation. God knows how to write straight with crooked lines, as the saying goes. But God's act of writing straight with crooked lines does not "straighten" these lines—it does not justify the evils of history by appealing to the goods that came out of them.

We would do well to follow the lead of Genesis. We ought to recognize both that striving for superiority can bring about important goods and that such striving is wrong and does significant harm. For if we occlude the evils of striving for superiority, we will never be able to abandon it in favor of a different striving, one that can drive genuine progress without being burdened by all the ills of striving for superiority: the kind of striving for excellence that is defined by purposes worthy of our God-given humanity.

# Conclusion

## Against Striving for Superiority—
## Twenty-Four Theses

**Clearing the Throat, and a Bit More—or What This Book Was About**

1. Striving for superiority is striving to be better than someone else—and, as a rule, to be recognized by others as better. Striving for superiority differs from striving for excellence, in which persons strive to achieve some good independently of how they compare with others. (For the distinction, see chapter 1.)

2. Striving for superiority can have—and has had—many positive effects. We owe to it, at least in part, many extraordinary advances in all fields of human endeavor: science, arts, sports, economy, and more. Still, striving for superiority is a vice. It is *morally* problematic for the strivers themselves, for their immediate surroundings, and for the world as a whole. (Rousseau's ambivalence about striving for superiority in chap. 1 is instructive.)

161

3. Striving for superiority comes in gradations of intensity, from tendencies that we observe in ourselves and are able to contain or overcome to an all-consuming hubristic passion to which we give ourselves over and which comes to possess us. Striving for superiority is at its worst when it becomes the dominant value to which most—and in extreme cases, all—other values are subordinated. It then becomes a nearly incurable vice. (Milton's Satan is the prime example.)

4. Striving for superiority is always an individual's striving. At the same time, it is an inherently *social* vice. By definition, it needs others whom a person can outdo. Mostly, it also feeds on the presence of a third party: on their gaze, assessment, and public recognition. Since recognition depends on a common public reference, striving for superiority presupposes a shared system of values in which being better than someone else is an important value. (Consider the standards of beauty in the case of Toni Morrison's Pecola or a vision of life "according to human standards" in Paul.)

5. People are often drawn into others' striving for superiority—attracted to become part of it, often seduced and sometimes forced into it. One way or another, their alleged superior greatness is folded into someone else's striving after it. Parents may push a child to strive for superiority in academic or athletic achievement to satisfy their own desire for superiority over their peers. Or energetic support of a political leader deemed superior— often a leader who makes outsized claims of their own superiority—may serve to shore up the standing of citizens who feel marginalized and inferior. (See Satan's bringing ruin to humans to win the superiority contest with God.)

**Superiority and Inferiority**

6. Much of the problematic nature of striving for superiority lies in the tendency to think that my being better than someone *at something* translates into my being better than they are *as a person*. A tacit assumption behind the sense of personal superiority is the idea that a person is the sum of their achievements and possessions; they are their own creation. Their achievements and possessions are who they *are*—and are therefore the measure of their worth as a person. (See the claim of Milton's Satan to self-creation.)

7. Throughout history, but perhaps especially today, many have come to believe that striving for superiority enhances the striving self. To the extent that it does, the cost of that enhancement to the self is significant. By elevating the striving self, it simultaneously devalues it, assuming it to be inferior, for the striving is predicated on a refusal to accept and to love the self if it does not measure up to or exceed its ubiquitous potential competitors. (Consider the self-loathing of Milton's Satan and the damage of comparisons in social media to children and teens; see chap. 1.)

8. It is not necessary—and it might not be possible—to determine which comes first: the desire to be superior or the pain of being inferior. The two mostly go together. Sustained striving to be superior is fueled by the pain of inferiority. At the same time, successful striving for superiority generates in its trail the disappointments of inferiority. (See the role of dejection in the striving of Kierkegaard's little lily and the consequences of the striving.)

9. Striving for superiority relieves the pain of the striver's inferiority by inferiorizing the one who has been bested; it is essentially about exchanging the positions of two competitors. Striving for superiority is seeking to offload the pain of inferiority onto another. It therefore displaces

rather than resolves the problem of inferiority. (Milton's Satan again is the prime example.)

10. It might seem that striving for superiority, if successful, would take care of the striver's sense of inferiority and increase their self-worth by giving them a sense of preeminence. But any sense of self-worth achieved in this way is fragile, always exposed to a takedown. Self-worth can be secured only when it does not derive from competitive relations—when it is established prior to all comparisons. (Kierkegaard claims that the lily would wither if it thought that it was loved by God not irrespective of its beauty but on account of it.)

11. The ugly underbelly of striving for superiority is that we might often seek to best our opponents by stymieing their efforts. I can achieve superiority over competitors by diminishing them and not just by improving myself. (That is the goal of Milton's Satan in rebelling against God, in tempting Adam, Eve, and Christ.)

## The Burden of Striving for Superiority

12. Because striving for superiority is tied not to a particular object, quality, or final destination but to besting the moving target of others' achievements, striving for superiority never comes to rest. Any superiority that we achieve is both hard-won and short-lived. Moreover, in striving for superiority we have to strive both to become superior and to remain superior; we can always fall behind, or others can catch up and overtake us. No matter how superior we become, the threat of inferiority looms. (Even GOATs can be GOATs for just one season.)

13. We tend to think of striving for superiority as an enactment of freedom: a sovereign individual pushing upward

to be the best. But when besting others is the most important—or even just the dominant—value, striving for superiority turns into compulsion. The pain of inferiority is too strong to endure, and we either fall into depression or *must* press upward to get relief from the sight of those we have vanquished. (Milton's Satan wages war against God while both knowing and suppressing the knowledge that he cannot win.)

14. In the grip of striving for superiority with no fixed destination or limit in sight, we have banished contentment from our lives. Restless, we find it easy to love and celebrate change, movement, and growth—or, at least, the appearance of growth—but we find it hard to love and celebrate what have been and have had, what we are and have, or even what we will be; the quest for superiority nearly always makes false promises about the future and so sets us up for disappointment. (Kierkegaard's little lily is the most vivid example.)

**Superiority, Truth, and Goodness**

15. Most claims to superiority rest on falsehood. None of my achievements are predominantly my own, and it is impossible to separate my contribution to them from those of many others. In whatever way I have proven to be superior at something over another person, I can never properly identify the extent to which I am the sole origin of that superiority and take credit for it myself. (For Paul, this is an important reason for the insufficiency of any comparative judgments about myself or others.)

16. Strivers for superiority often deploy falsehood as a weapon against competitors; sometimes what they think

is true about themselves and others is in fact a distortion or denial of truth. In seeking recognition of my superiority and in avoiding the shame of inferiority, I exaggerate my achievements and diminish those of others. Falsehoods and lies lift me higher in the perception of others than my achievements alone could, even as my very claim to these achievements already rested in part on falsehood, as I noted in thesis 15. (For the role of falsehood in striving for superiority, consider Milton's Satan.)

17. When being superior to others is the dominant value, striving for superiority empties many genuine goods of value. Their value is then indexed to their contribution to the striver's superiority; every good has only an instrumental value, no matter how valuable or even holy it might be in itself. (This is one lesson from Paul's "rubbishing" of God's law in using it as an instrument of his own superior self-righteousness, or from Kierkegaard's little lily's trashing of its own beauty, which was greater than Solomon's glory.) If a good thing marks me as inferior because my competitor has acquired a better thing and achieved more, that very fact will devalue that good in my eyes as merely a failed means to my end. Conversely, if a genuine good marks my competitor as superior, it will be difficult, and at times impossible, for me to delight in that good. (Milton's Satan, observing the newly created earth, is "undelighted" in all the "delight" of its beauty.)

18. The inferiority that striving for superiority unleashes has had devastating consequences on the biosphere. To climb in social hierarchy we enter the wasteful cycle of discarding anything that sets us back—last year's fashion item or a two-year-old smartphone—and acquire new things that enhance our status, all the while "rubbishing" our planetary home. Striving for superiority that

accelerates innovation makes us not only blind to many noncompetitive goods—like kāhuli tree snails, the "jewels of the forest"—but turns us into active agents of their destruction.

19. Striving for superiority tends to erase the particularities of persons. A striver for superiority mostly makes comparisons on a single scale of value—a single kind of beauty, a single kind of intelligence, a single measure of success, and so on—and then seeks to instantiate a higher form of that value than others. In the process, we betray our own specific form of being human, the kind of beauty, intelligence, and success that are appropriate specifically to us. At the same time, by focusing on ranking, a striver for superiority loses a sense of glory of the sheer fact that they are humans. Striving for superiority, we "die," "killed" by our own hand, which is pushed to the ghastly deed by the culture and structure of striving for superiority. (Kierkegaard highlights the dangers both to our uniqueness and to our common humanity.)

**Beyond Superiority and Inferiority**

20. To avoid "dying"—to live in true freedom and with joy—we must give up on striving for superiority. Each of us is glorious by simply being human. God gives us each both being and glory by bringing us into existence as a unique specimen of humanity. When others break us and we break ourselves, whether by striving for superiority or in other ways, God promises to make us into a "new creation." On account of God's valuing of us and standing by us whether we are broken or whole, our glory is greater than anything we can do to make ourselves glorious. (That is Paul's, Milton's, and Kierkegaard's key conviction, the foundation of the entire edifice of their thought.)

21. The standing of any person in community is exactly equal to the standing of any other; there are no superior and inferior members. Superior and inferior worth or status are social fictions—powerfully attractive and highly destructive fictions, but fictions nonetheless. (Paul is clear, and Kierkegaard adamant, about this.)

22. Our God-given glory is both the destination reached and the journey begun. It is the call of our very being to live into and enact in the world our own particular glory as God's unique and irreplaceable creature. This is an invitation to striving, to zeal even. But in this striving, it does not matter how we stack up against others. Others are not our measures, though they can be our inspirations or warnings. The measure of excellence is Jesus Christ. And he is also the guarantee of our future excellence (a point on which Paul, Milton, and Kierkegaard insist).

23. One of the most revolutionary injunctions in the New Testament—a key aspect of the excellence to which the followers of Christ should aspire—is that each person in a community should treat all others as if they were superior to themselves, superior not in achievement but in importance. Obedience to this injunction is likely the best way to subvert striving for superiority and the resulting hierarchies of honor, which all depend more on relative than absolute differences.

24. The practice of treating others as superior to us is more than just a strategy for radical social change. It reflects the very character of the God from whom, through whom, and for whom are all things (Rom. 11:36). In Jesus Christ, as the Nicene Creed puts it, the One "through whom all things were made . . . came down"—and became a servant, even of the humblest of humans, so as to elevate them all to his own kind of glory.

# Acknowledgments

I believe that we are opaque to ourselves—"we are unknown to ourselves, we knowers," writes Nietzsche (*On the Genealogy of Morality*)—and that others are even less knowable to us. We therefore don't really know the extent to which any of our achievements are properly our own and how much we owe to others (see chap. 4, sec. 6). If this is true, writing acknowledgments is a hopeless endeavor. And yet it is necessary, and not entirely impossible. Fear not, I will not try to trace all the contributions of others to this work, starting with what happened in the mind of God before this universe burst into existence with a flash of light, according to both modern science and ancient Genesis (as Marilynne Robinson notes in *Reading Genesis*). That would be the "impossible" part of the "not entirely impossible." What is possible is to name contributors who have directly helped in crafting this book. It is my duty and joy to name them even if I cannot identify precisely where my contribution ends and theirs begins. We rightly insist on honoring the author, but we really don't know what it means to be an author of a work, who or what exactly is the author of a book—"author," that is, in the original sense of the originator, "creator, one who brings about, one who makes or creates" (Online Etymology Dictionary).

As a general acknowledgment, I can say that this book about striving for superiority, even if it turns out to be good, does not establish any identifiable marginal superiority of its author over anyone. Any boast about it would be spread very widely, and I cannot tell what slice of it is my own. I did write most of its words and compose most of its paragraphs, except for those I indicated were authored by Taylor Craig, my excellent research assistant to whom I am deeply grateful for the work he did on this book. He helped me think through both the substance and the form of the book, shortened the Milton chapter and helped divide the chapter on Paul into two, all of which involved some writing as well, unacknowledged in the text of the book. At one stage in the writing process, Eric Holland did excellent work as my research assistant as well. I am grateful also to Karin Fransen (of the Yale Center for Faith & Culture) for her editorial work. Some of the words in the book are hers, and the absence of a few misspelled words, wrongly chosen words, and clumsily constructed sentences can be traced back to her as well. Eric Salo (of Baker) ably prepared the manuscript for print.

Many colleagues and friends have read previous versions of individual chapters or the whole manuscript and offered valuable comments: Drew Collins, Matthew Croasmun, Andrew Davison, Keri Day, Jeffrey Dill, Filippo Falcone, Matteo Frey, Stephen Garcia, John Hare, Justin Hawkins, Jeppe Hedaa, Peter Johnson, Francisco Javier López Frías, Ross McCullough, Teresa Morgan, Stephanie Mota Thurston, Tiago de Melo Novais, Charlotte vanOyen-Witvliet, Mark Seifrid, Kendall Soulen, Kathryn Tanner, and Jonathan Wilson-Hartgrove. It was Jonathan who nudged me to write directly about what Jesus had to say about striving for superiority, rather than merely let Milton and Kierkegaard articulate it. The result is the first part of chapter 6.

Looking at the manuscript of this book, I am grateful to the members of the advisory board of the Yale Center for Faith & Culture: Marjie Calvert, Meagan Carter, Smoot Carter, Bill Cross,

Laura Giles, Walter Giles, Julie Johnson, Louis Kim, Pam King, Patty Love, Skip Masback, Peter Meringolo, Jill Otto, Fred Sievert, Beth Stephenson, and Scott Stephenson. Without them, I would not have a staff, some of whom were among those who researched, edited, and commented on drafts of this book. I tried the ideas for the book on all board members, and with some of them I had longer exchanges about its thesis.

I delivered some of the book's content as the Richard Myers Lecture Series at University Baptist Church in Charlottesville, Virginia (2022), as the Gross Memorial Lectures at Valparaiso University, Valparaiso, Indiana (2024), and as the Edward Schillebeecx Lecture at the Catholic University of Leuven, Belgium (2024). I am grateful to Matthew Tennant, Lisa Driver, and Stephan van Erp for the invitations and to the audiences at these lectures for active engagement with the material. As I noted in the preface, a very early form of the material was first presented at the Second Global Congress on Sport and Christianity at Calvin University, Grand Rapids, Michigan (2019). I am grateful to Brian Bolt for inviting me, to Kristen Deede Johnson for her response, and to a group of faculty who later came to the discussion of the lecture and of my theology more broadly. It is partly because of their pushback that my first effort to write about striving for superiority could mature into this book.

Over the years, the McDonald Agape Foundation has supported my work and the work of the Yale Center for Faith & Culture. It also directly funded two small conferences at Yale about striving for superiority, allowing me to handpick colleagues to help me think through various aspects of the issue. I am grateful in particular to Peter McDonald, the foundation's current president, and the members of its board for believing in the work I am doing.

Robert Hosack, my editor at Brazos, deserves gratitude not just for shepherding this book through the editorial process but also for allowing me to substitute this book for another to which I obliged myself contractually.

The book is dedicated to Ryan MacAnnally-Linz, current managing director of the Yale Center for Faith & Culture. He became my research assistant shortly after he came from Dartmouth to study at Yale Divinity School in 2008, and we have been collaborating ever since. Because he wrote a fine doctoral dissertation on humility, he was the first person I talked to when, in 2018, I started working on a lecture on striving for superiority for the Global Congress on Sport and Christianity. We discussed the idea during a long car ride; I remember the discussion, but not where we were going or why. More than anyone else I know well, he embodies the disinterest in striving for superiority and the zeal for excellence that this book seeks to articulate and promote.

Finally and most importantly, I am deeply grateful to my wife Jessica and my daughter Mira. Each in her own way is a source of strength and joy—and they are much-needed and welcome reminders that, as the apostle Paul writes, we love each other well when we seek to hold each other to be more important than ourselves.

# Notes

Preface

1. Taylor, *Cosmic Connections*, 572.

Chapter 1 "O Solomon, I Have Outdone You!"

1. For a brief historical overview, see Ousterhout, *Eastern Medieval Architecture*, chap. 9. I am grateful to Vasileios Marinis for pointing me to this and several other sources in this section.

2. Harrison, "Church of St. Polyeuktos," 279.

3. Harrison, "Church of St. Polyeuktos," 278.

4. Bardill, "New Temple for Byzantium," 343.

5. McClanan, *Representations of Early Byzantine Empresses*, 94–98.

6. McClanan, *Representations of Early Byzantine Empresses*, 96–97.

7. Barker, *Justinian and the Later Roman Empire*, 183.

8. Schibille, *Hagia Sophia*, 124–28. I owe this reference to Felicity Harley-McGowan. See also Ousterhout, *Eastern Medieval Architecture*, 206.

9. Paul the Silentiary, "Description of Hagia Sophia," in Bell, *Three Political Voices*, 197.

10. Ousterhout, *Eastern Medieval Architecture*, 203, 207–8.

11. Ousterhout, *Eastern Medieval Architecture*, 210.

12. When Sultan Mehmet II conquered Constantinople almost nine hundred years later in 1453, he turned it into a mosque, which, with a brief interruption, it remains to this day. As a church, it called into question the greatness of Islam. In 1616, Sultan Ahmed I built the magnificent Blue Mosque across from Hagia Sophia to overshadow it. (On the legal validity of keeping Hagia Sophia a mosque, see "Hagia Sophia Case.")

13. The question remains how exactly to fit the splendor of Hagia Sophia with Paul's theology of the cross, his resistance to the "superiority of words or wisdom," during the pilgrimage to the future glory. See chap. 4.

14. See Frías, "Games as Windows and Remedies."

15. Quoted in Sandel, *Tyranny of Merit*, 71.

16. Wallace, *This Is Water*, 3–4.

17. Quoted in Nietzsche, "Homer's Contest," in *On the Genealogy of Morality*, 189–90.

18. For the more traditional view that stresses the dangers of *amour propre*, see Charvet, *Social Problem in the Philosophy of Jean-Jacques Rousseau*. For the revisionist view, which stresses its possible constructive manifestations, see Neuhouser, *Rousseau's Theodicy of Self-Love*.

19. Bertram, "Jean-Jacques Rousseau."

20. Rousseau, "Discourse on the Origin and the Foundation of Inequality among Men or Second Discourse," 224 (hereafter, *Second Discourse*).

21. Rousseau, *Second Discourse*, 170.

22. Under the influence of Rousseau, but with a more sophisticated anthropology in which a distinction is made between human predisposition and propensity toward evil, Immanuel Kant traces the origin of envy—and consequent striving for superiority, though striving for superiority is not what he stresses—to the presence of other human beings, not as bad examples that lead others astray but simply by their presence. Human needs, Kant thinks, "are but limited, and his state of mind in providing for them moderate and tranquil." Yet the presence of others introduces dissatisfaction. "He is poor (or considers himself so) only to the extent that he is anxious that other human beings will consider him poor and will despise him for it." Kant, *Religion within the Boundaries of Mere Reason*, 105.

23. Rousseau, *Second Discourse*, 170.

24. Rousseau, *Second Discourse*, 189.

25. Rousseau, *Second Discourse*, 189 (emphasis added).

26. Rousseau, *Second Discourse*, 171.

27. Meier, "Rousseaus Disckurs über den Ursprung," lxv, lxxin72.

28. Rousseau, *Second Discourse*, 192–93.

29. Smith, *Theory of Moral Sentiments*, 57–58.

30. Unlike other animals, humans have "no other goal, nor other garland, but being the foremost." Hobbes, *Elements of Law*, 36, 47.

31. Rosa, *Resonance*, 1. On the opening page of *Resonance*, he summarizes his argument in *Social Acceleration* as follows: the "social formation of modernity"—in economy, politics, science, arts—"cannot stabilize itself except dynamically. . . . [It] must forever be expanding, growing and innovating, increasing production and consumption as well as options and opportunities for connection."

32. Plato, too, believed that human desires, specifically the desire to become rich, is "insatiable." Plato, *Republic* 555b, in *Plato: Complete Works*, 1166.

33. Galbraith, *Affluent Society*, 155, 153.

34. Ehrenberg, *Weariness of the Self*. As Byung-Chul Han has pointed out, Ehrenberg overlooks systemic causes of depression, economic pressures to be better than others, and the causes of social fragmentation that leave us bereft of resources to cope with depression. Han, *Burnout Society*, 9–11.

35. This section was drafted by Taylor Craig.

36. US Surgeon's General Advisory, *Social Media and Youth Mental Health*.

37. US Surgeon's General Advisory, *Social Media and Youth Mental Health*, 8.

38. Luthar and Kumar, "Youth in High-Achieving Schools," 441.

39. Luthar and Kumar, "Youth in High-Achieving Schools," 441.

40. Sandel, *Tyranny of Merit*, 7.

41. Sandel, *Tyranny of Merit*, 10–11.

42. For the report, see Kavanagh and Rich, *Truth Decay*. For news coverage, see Jennifer Kavanagh and Michael D. Rich, "The 'Truth Decay' Research That Made

Obama's Reading List," CNN, June 21, 2018, https://www.cnn.com/2018/06/19
/opinions/truth-decay-opinion-rich-kavanagh/index.html.
43. Kavanagh and Rich, *Truth Decay*, iii.
44. Janezic and Gallego, "Eliciting Preferences for Truth-Telling."
45. Rousseau, *Second Discourse*, 170.
46. For a discussion of possible evolutionary foundations of the striving for superiority, see, e.g., Chapais, "Competence and the Evolutionary Origins of Status"; and Cheng, Tracy, and Henrich, "Pride, Personality, and the Evolutionary Foundations."
47. I owe the idea that striving for excellence can take the form of striving not to get worse to Ryan McAnnally-Linz.
48. Striving for superiority plays a crucial role in the psychology of Alfred Adler. But he uses "striving for superiority" to designate what I call striving for excellence. For him, it is the fundamental driver of human behavior, a way for a person to actualize their own "self-ideal": "The striving for superiority never ceases. It constitutes in fact the mind, the psyche of the individual. As we have said, life is the attainment of a goal or form, and it is the striving for superiority which sets the attainment of form into motion" (Adler, *Best of Alfred Adler*, 334). Though striving for superiority, as Adler understands it, can express itself in competitive behaviors, unlike for me, it is not for him essentially a striving "to be better than" someone else. When competition is involved, as in the lives of second-born children, he describes it as striving for superiority "under steam" (164). For him, striving for superiority is about overcoming a sense of lack, improving the perceived lot in life, coming closer to the self-ideal rather than outdoing someone else, as it is for me. As such, it is "universal," just as the feeling of inferiority is universal (325). I use the phrase in a more restricted sense than Adler does.
49. Striving for excellence, I may in fact end up being the best. For business, see the case of Warren Buffett in Walter, "Case against Competing." For sports, see Hawkins, "Pusillanimity, Superiority, Magnanimity, Haecceity."
50. These sentences are an edited version of a comment on an earlier version of this text by Frías, "Games as Windows and Remedies."
51. For examples from the 2024 Summer Olympics, see Brad Stulberg, "What the Olympics Can Teach Us about Excellence," *New York Times*, August 11, 2024, https://www.nytimes.com/2024/08/09/opinion/paris-olympics-gold-excellence.html.
52. I owe this formulation to Taylor Craig.
53. With a slight change, the formulation comes from Soulen, untitled paper, 1.
54. Stephen L. Darwall, "Two Kinds of Respect," *Ethics* 88, no. 1 (1977), 36–49.
55. Smith, *Theory of Moral Sentiments*, 58.
56. See Cortina, *Aporophobia*.
57. This section was drafted by Taylor Craig.
58. This section was drafted by Taylor Craig.
59. Several commentators have read the *Paradise Lost* and *Paradise Regained* cycle as a fundamental contrast between the humility of the Son and the pride of Satan. *Paradise Lost* 3.303–322 is a sustained and direct reference to the Carmen Christi of Philippians 2. This is a foundational text for the structure of the whole poem, as it lays out the plan of redemption as agreed to by the Father and the Son. In addition, Christ's humility in the incarnation is prefigured by his humility in being numbered with the angels as their king (5.843)—and so it is actually a movement of divine humility that sparks Satan's proud revolt. See Barnaby, "Form of a Servant"; Labriola, "'Thy Humiliation Shall Exalt'"; Hunter, "Milton on the Exaltation of the Son"; and Johnston, "Milton on the Doctrine of the Atonement." I am grateful to Filippo Falcone, who pointed me to several

of these references and who added his opinion that 3.303–322 is "absolutely central to *Paradise Lost* and its structure" in personal correspondence (November 27, 2023).

60. Kierkegaard, Upbuilding Discourses, 169.

61. Kierkegaard, *Philosophical Fragments*, 42.

## Chapter 2 The Worry of Comparison (Kierkegaard)

1. Kierkegaard, *Upbuilding Discourses*, 169.

2. Kierkegaard, *Upbuilding Discourses*, 167, 168, 169.

3. See Löwith, *Von Hegel zu Nietzsche*, 125–30.

4. Kierkegaard, *Works of Love*, 70.

5. Kierkegaard, *Works of Love*, 70.

6. See Kierkegaard, *Upbuilding Discourses*, 167, 169.

7. For a contemporary advocate of a position close to one of Kierkegaard rejects, see de Benoist, *On Being a Pagan*.

8. Kierkegaard, *Upbuilding Discourses*, 69.

9. Kierkegaard, *Works of Love*, 67.

10. See especially his *Works of Love*. Kierkegaard finished *Works of Love* in September 1847. *Upbuilding Discourses*, where he uses lilies and birds to discuss the worry of comparison, was written six months earlier (March 1847), and *Christian Discourses*, where he discusses the worry of lowliness and the worry of loftiness, was written seven months after *Works of Love* (April 1848). All three books were published under his own name, indicating that he identified fully with their content.

11. Unlike Rousseau, Kierkegaard is not offering here a genetic account of the striving for superiority. He is analyzing striving for superiority as a prevalent mode of sinning against God and neighbor.

12. Kierkegaard, *Upbuilding Discourses*, 165.

13. Kierkegaard, *Upbuilding Discourses*, 169.

14. Kierkegaard, *Upbuilding Discourses*, 161.

15. Kierkegaard, *Works of Love*, 69.

16. See Löwith, *Von Hegel zu Nietzsche*, 175.

17. Kierkegaard, *Upbuilding Discourses*, 189.

18. Kierkegaard, *Upbuilding Discourses*, 171.

19. Kierkegaard, *Upbuilding Discourses*, 189.

20. Kierkegaard, *Upbuilding Discourses*, 179.

21. Kierkegaard, *Upbuilding Discourses*, 165.

22. Kierkegaard, *Christian Discourses*, 40.

23. Kierkegaard, *Upbuilding Discourses*, 165.

24. Kierkegaard, *Sickness unto Death*, 13–14 (emphasis added).

25. Kierkegaard, *Sickness unto Death*, 14.

26. Kierkegaard, *Sickness unto Death*, 15.

27. Kierkegaard, *Sickness unto Death*, 14.

28. Kierkegaard, *Works of Love*, 71. See also Kierkegaard, *Upbuilding Discourses*, 171: "To be a human being is not lower than diversities but is raised above them, inasmuch as this, the essentially equal glory among all human beings . . . is their equality in loveliness."

29. Kierkegaard, *Christian Discourses*, 58.

30. Morrison, *Bluest Eye*. The term "racial self-loathing" is Morrison's; she uses it of Pecola in a 1993 foreword to the book, more than twenty years after its original publication (xi).

31. Kierkegaard, *Christian Discourses*, 58.

32. Simmel, *Schriften zur Soziologie*, 171.

33. Kierkegaard, *Christian Discourses*, 37–38.

34. Kierkegaard, *Works of Love*, 71.

35. Kierkegaard, *Christian Discourses*, 37–38.

36. Kierkegaard, *Christian Discourses*, 38.

37. Kierkegaard, *Philosophical Fragments*, 36–37.

38. On the care of loftiness, see Kierkegaard, *Christian Discourses*, 48–59.

39. Kierkegaard, *Sickness unto Death*, 14.

40. In Lippitt and Evans, "Søren Kierkegaard," the authors note that, for Kierkegaard, a self is not "a kind of metaphysical substance, but rather more like an achievement, a goal to strive for" (sec. 2). The denial is correct, but the affirmation that it is an achievement is misleading, even if it is qualified with "more like." I think that it occludes what, for Kierkegaard, is most important, which is that God is the power that establishes the self so that the self's achievement is above all to "rest transparently" in the reality of having been established and act in freedom out of that rest.

41. Kierkegaard, *Christian Discourses*, 42.

42. See Roberts, *Recovering Christian Character*, 308.

43. Kierkegaard, *Christian Discourses*, 50.

44. Kierkegaard, *Works of Love*, 72.

45. Kierkegaard, *Christian Discourses*, 37.

46. Kierkegaard, *Without Authority*, 130, 129.

47. As Kierkegaard sees it, even the tax collector, had he compared himself with the Pharisee and found himself wanting, would also have measured himself wrongly; he would have engaged in the same comparative moral calculus among dissimilar people and judged himself as failing. But the tax collector is standing with his guilt *before* God rather than before the Pharisee—and ends up, just for that reason, justified.

48. Kierkegaard, *Upbuilding Discourses*, 159–82.

49. Kierkegaard, *Sickness unto Death*, supplement, 158.

50. Kierkegaard, *Christian Discourses*, 130–31.

51. Kierkegaard, *Practice in Christianity*, 241.

52. Kierkegaard, *Upbuilding Discourses*, 199.

53. Kierkegaard, *Upbuilding Discourses*, 200.

54. As far as I can tell, Kierkegaard never discussed whether there may be forms of distinctiveness that cannot and ought not be worn lightly because they deeply define us.

55. Kierkegaard, *Christian Discourses*, 55.

56. Kierkegaard, *Christian Discourses*, 54. In the section of *Christian Discourses* from which I am quoting, Kierkegaard is seeking to answer a puzzling question—namely, why is it, as the Gospels consistently claim, *not* "just as easy and just as difficult for the lowly one to become a Christian as it is for the eminent." After all, the lowliness that is required from both "is not the external but the internal, a feeling of one's own lowlines, which the eminent can have just as well as the lowly." Kierkegaard, *Christian Discourses*, 54.

57. Kierkegaard, *Works of Love*, 81–82.

58. Kierkegaard, *Works of Love*, 82.

59. Kierkegaard, *Works of Love*, 67.

60. Kierkegaard, *Works of Love*, 84.

61. Kierkegaard, *Works of Love*, 83–85.

62. Kierkegaard, *Works of Love*, 88. Clearly, dissimilarities of individual particularities, of the individual essence, cannot hang loosely on the individual. Social dissimilarities can and should, Kierkegaard thinks.

63. For an argument that Kierkegaard's social criticism is often underappreciated, see Plekon, "Moral Accounting."

## Chapter 3 Satan's Aspiration (Milton)

1. Milton, "Tenure of Kings and Magistrates," 754.
2. Lewis, *Preface to Paradise Lost*, 72.
3. Lewis, *Preface to Paradise Lost*, 93. See also Cohen, "Injured Merit."
4. Kierkegaard, *Christian Discourses*, 130–31. See also chap. 2 herein.
5. Milton's Christology is a matter of some scholarly debate. Much discussion centers on the question of *De Doctrina Christiana*, a work often accused of christological Arianism and typically attributed to Milton. The authorship of this piece, however, has been the subject of much debate (for recent reviews, see Urban, "Revisiting the History of the *De Doctrina Christiana* Authorship Debate"; and Urban, "Increasing Distance between *De Doctrina Christiana* and Milton's Poetry"). Without taking a decided position on the question of authorship, I share Urban's sense that we can most fruitfully read *Paradise Lost* by not constraining it in advance to share the Christology of *De Doctrina Christiana*. For the purposes of my argument, the most important consideration is that Milton's Satan, especially in his soliloquy in book 4, does not base his argument on the creation in time of the Son, a fact that would surely be relevant and even decisive if Satan believed in it. My argument will therefore proceed on the premise that the Son in *Paradise Lost* is fairly read as being a co-Creator with the Father. (This footnote was composed by Taylor Craig.)
6. Rogers, in *"Paradise Lost*: Books V–VI," takes Satan at his word that Abdiel's account of angelic creation is a "strange point and new" (*PL* 5:805) and tries to make plausible Satan's account of angelic self-creation. He also takes the Father's words "This day I have begot whom I declare / My only son, and on this holy hill / Him has anointed, whom ye now behold" (*PL* 5:603–4) to refer to the *creation* of the Son rather than to his appointment to rule as a vicegerent. If Rogers is right, the Father's elevation of the Son is arbitrary, and Satan is right to complain about God's injustice. One might wonder whether *Paradise Lost* is here being read as if the christological Arianism of *De Doctrina Christiana* must be its interpretive key rather than being read simply on its own terms. As we will see shortly, in the famous soliloquy in book 4, Satan recognizes that God created him and gave him eminence. Satan has immediate military and political interest in denying his and the angels' creation by God, in being "forgetful" that he received existence and eminence from God (*PL* 4:54). In his soliloquy, in which he affirms emphatically that he is a creature of God, he has no interest in making *this* affirmation. In fact, he would be better off if he could deny having been created, as the reality of being a creature, and therefore inferior to God, is the main source of his torment there.
7. Rogers takes the idea of "self-creation" to be the ontological foundation of egalitarianism. But that is to see things from Satan's perspective: the claim to equality with God requires the idea of self-creation. Self-creation can hardly ground equality among ensuing entities. For Milton, God's creation is the ground of egalitarianism among humans.
8. The first part of the soliloquy (*PL* 4:33–41) was written "several years before the poem was begun." Phillips, *Life of Milton*, 1034.
9. Nietzsche, *On the Genealogy of Morality* 1.10.
10. "Unbounded hope" is equivalent to being "enthralled / By sin to foul exorbitant desires" (*PL* 3:176–77).
11. In addressing the Son, who will be opposing Satan, the Father notes that Satan not only wants "to erect his throne / Equal to ours, throughout the spacious North" but also aims to conquer "this our high place, our sanctuary, our hill" (*PL* 5:725–32).

12. After Satan enters the serpent and is about to begin the work of temptation, he reflects on the beauty of the earth, noting that "the more I see / Pleasures about me, so much more I feel / Torment within me." He goes on to say that "in Heav'n much worse would be my state" and then states, "But neither here seek I, nor in Heav'n / To dwell, unless by maistring Heav'n's Supreme" (*PL* 9:119–25). The entire misery of Satan stems from not being supreme. Even in destruction of the earth he aims to best God:

> To me shall be the glory sole among
> Th'infernal Powers, in one day to have marr'd
> What the Almighty styl'd, six Nights and Days
> Continu'd making, and who knows how long
> Before had be contriving. (*PL* 9:135–39)

In destroying, he is greater than God in creating.

13. On the acknowledgment account of gratitude, see Volf and McAnnally-Linz, "Joyful Recognition."

14. One can see an analogous example of both knowing and not knowing—desperately needing not to know—in Satan's relation to God's power, though in this case the interest is generating hope in his defeated troops and maintaining hope in himself that they "shall not fail to reascend / Self-raised, and repossess their native seat," which they lost after being driven out of heaven. Speaking of God, he tells his troops, "But he who reigns Monarch in Heav'n, till then as one secure / Sat on his throne, upheld by old repute, / Consent or custom, and his regal state / Put forth at full, but still his strength concealed, / Which tempted our attempt, and wrought our fall" (*PL* 1:637–42). In Satan's portrayal, the lack of a display of God's power in heaven is not an expression of the fact that God values power less than love but a mere trick to ferret out disloyal denizens of heaven so as to exile them from his realm.

15. Early in *Paradise Lost*, after Satan and his army are routed out of heaven and hurled into hell, Satan boasts that he "shook his [God's] throne" and that, at the terror of Satan's arm, God "doubted [feared for] his empire" (*PL* 1:105, 113–15). Some interpreters suggest that Satan is actually persuaded that he struck God with terror and that God's power is exaggerated. If so, that could only be a result of self-delusion. It is hard, though, to imagine that Satan, of all creatures, does not know the extent of God's power. After all, he calls him "the Omnipotent" (*PL* 4:86). It is more likely that he is inflating his power and diminishing God's, given that he is speaking these words to his second in command, trying to justify the rebellion that ended in an inglorious defeat and to motivate him to continue the struggle. To do anything less would be to admit failure, to give up on the striving to best God. Hence the public boast—namely, that he can subdue God (*PL* 4:86–92). Contrary to Rogers, Satan offers no demystification of God's power here; he is throwing wool over the eyes of his subordinates, trying to salvage his own reputation by telling what he knows are lies. That's why he claims that God, who "sat on his throne, upheld by old repute, / Consent or custom" has tricked them into rebellion. God was "tempting our attempt" by concealing his power and so "wrought our fall" (*PL* 1:639–43). All of this is bluster and obfuscation against his own better judgment in order to salvage his ruined reputation. After all, he is the ruler in hell, and his rule depends on his subordinates' faith in his power.

16. The sentiment is not obvious. Achilles, for instance, would rather be a paid servant in the poor man's house than the king of kings among the dead. See Homer, *Odyssey*, 11:489–91.

17. For a seminal reading of Milton's treatment of Eve, see Gilbert, "Patriarchal Poetry and Women Readers."

18. Milton is following closely, though, the original story of Narcissus, who, like Eve, is at first not aware that he is beholding a reflection of his own image. See Kilgour, "'Thy Perfect Image Viewing.'" For Narcissus, see Ovid's description in *Metamorphoses*, 3:339–510.

19. Corresponding to the comparative "less" adjectives that Eve uses to describe Adam in relation to herself, we have in book 8 "less" adverbs that Adam uses to describe Eve in relation to himself:

> At least on her bestowed
> Too much of ornament, in outward show
> Elaborate, of inward less exact.
> For well I understand in the prime end
> Of Nature her th' inferior, in the mind
> And inward faculties, which most excel,
> In outward also her resembling less
> His image who made both, and less expressing
> The character of that dominion giv'n
> O'er other creatures. (*PL* 8:537–46)

20. See *Areopagitica*, in Milton, *Complete Poems*, 733: "If every action, which is good or evil in man at ripe years, were to be under pittance and prescription and compulsion, what were virtue but a name, what praise could be then due to well-doing, what gramercy to be sober, just, or continent?"

21. Milton seems to have shared with St. Augustine (*City of God*, 14.11), and much of the Christian tradition until the middle of the last century, the prejudice that women are intellectually inferior to men and that their intellectual inferiority is a result of their divinely created and unchangeable nature.

22. She was innocent in that discomfort because she did not act on it. For Milton, feeling attraction to something one ought not do, to be tempted to do it, does not take one out of the state of innocence. To commit sin, you must actually do the forbidden thing to which you are attracted, and therefore tempted, to do. On this, see Falcone, *Milton's Inward Liberty*.

23. "Secondness" is Sandra Gilbert's term for what I have described as "inferiority." That is what Eve was rebelling against, Gilbert rightly notes. Gilbert, "Patriarchal Poetry and Women Readers," 370.

My question is this: What was the positive goal that guided her rebellion? One option is equality, and the other is superiority. I argue that, though she may have started the rebellion in the name of equality, Satan's cunning expanded her aspiration to superiority.

24. See Falcone, *Milton's Inward Liberty*, 141–42. This seems also to have been Satan's position, though addressing the rebellious angelic hosts—Thrones, Dominions, Princedoms, Virtues, Powers—he suggests that, though they are not equal to him, yet they are "free, / Equally free" (*PL* 5:791–92). But he is invested in his own superiority, and to affirm him as supreme, they need to believe what he does not believe—namely, that freedom and inequality are compatible.

25. With the help of Satan, she thinks she has become superior not just to Adam but to Satan himself, the most eminent among God's creatures before his fall; she is, he flatters her, to be above all angels, "of right declared / Sov'reign of creatures, universal dame" (*PL* 9:611–12). The Tempter has crafted her into his own image. Having fled from her secondness, her inferiority to Adam, she, in her imagination, has reached the pinnacle of creaturely superiority. Her ambition is unlike Satan's only in that she is not seeking to best God.

26. C. S. Lewis goes too far in claiming that, in deciding to let Adam share in the fruit, Eve actually decides to commit murder (Lewis, *Preface to Paradise Lost*, 121). Though fearing that she may die for disobeying God's sole command, she is still hoping that the tree will deliver what the serpent said it would. She thinks her odds are good, for the serpent ate from the tree and did not die. That's why she worships the tree before she returns to Adam: "But first low reverence done, as to the power / That dwelt within, whose presence had infused / Into the plant sciential sap, derived / From nectar, drink of gods" (*PL* 9:835–38). She fears death but bets on elevation—and wants Adam to bet with her just in case her bet proves wrongly placed. If she does not share fruit and God finds that out, she will die, which, from the perspective of the living, is the state of ultimate inferiority.

27. Plutarch, "Caesar," sec. 11.

28. On Jesus seeking to glorify those he came to redeem, see Milton, "On the Morning of Christ's Nativity," in *Complete Poems*, 42–49.

29. Blake, *Marriage of Heaven and Hell*, 10.

30. Pattison, "Milton," chap. 2.

31. In the following comments on the poem, I lean on Rogers, "Infant Cry of God."

32. This is taken from Milton's description of the purpose of the nativity ode in "Elegy VI," written to his friend Charles Diodati. Milton, *Complete Poems*, 52.

33. Milton, "Elegy VI," in *Complete Poems*, 52.

34. Milton, "Elegy VI," in *Complete Poems*, 52.

35. In personal correspondence responding to an earlier version of this text, Filippo Falcone pushes against this reading of the nativity ode: "I have always regarded this as a paradox of love—to be first in love is for the self to lag behind. If the pagan Magi are on their way to honor the God who became a baby, the first who became last, how much more should Milton be one to outrun them, mindful that the one who is first is a servant of all. To be the first at the Savior's crib is to fully embrace the theology of God's weakness." Falcone, email message to author, September 25, 2023. This is a possible reading. What prevents me from embracing it is that Milton's self does not seem to be lagging behind; it is in the foreground, given his striving to be the first. Milton seems here like the sons of Zebedee, James and John, each wanting to be elevated above others by sitting one to Jesus's left and the other to Jesus's right in his glory, a request Jesus rejects—along with the indignation of the rest of the disciples against the two strivers for superiority—and then goes on to connect greatness not to elevation to the highest position but to service (Mark 10:35–45).

36. Milton, "Elegy VI," in *Complete Poems*, 53.

37. Rogers, "Infant Cry of God" (emphasis added).

38. To Milton's credit, he borrowed freely and extensively from others and mastered "the anxiety of being belated, preceded, and preempted" with ease (Kerrigan, Rumrich, and Fallon, introduction to *Paradise Lost*, by Milton, xliii). (After all, the stories told by these two poems were hardly original!) Harold Bloom has argued that Satan represents the poet afraid to show his debts, afraid of citation, afraid of being derivative—the modern poet—whereas Milton leans into the ways his work builds on the work of others, and his art is all the better for it (Bloom, *Anxiety of Influence*, 20–21). If so, all this may be a witness to his attempts to resist the temptation of striving for superiority.

## Chapter 4 "Outdo One Another in Showing Honor" (Paul)

1. Theissen, *Religion of the Earliest Churches*, 13–14, 63–64, 101.

2. Paul was an engaged and situational thinker. I will therefore need to piece together various aspects of his critique and of the proposed alternative from his letters: mainly Romans, 1 and 2 Corinthians, and Philippians. (The risk of such a "unified" reading is that of leveling contextually and biographically conditioned differences. I find, across his corpus, shifts of emphasis but a reasonably unified position, marked by a tension in his account of agency.) Paul is, I think, also one of those situational thinkers who is systematic as well. Still, there are tensions, two of which have a bearing on our topic. One is his account of the relationship between grace and human agency, especially with regard to the day of judgment. The other is between his affirmation of egalitarianism before God and in the church and his affirmation of hierarchy in broader social relations. Since I don't think these tensions can be fully resolved, in offering a sketch of his position on striving for superiority, I will rely on what I think is the dominant strand of his thought: the affirmation of radical grace and of egalitarian relations. The sketch would change, though not fundamentally, if I incorporated (1) a marginal strand in which he seems to advocate for cooperation of humans with God in salvation (see Rom. 2:6–8) into my argument—getting in by faith, staying in by divinely aided works—and (2) his affirmation of hierarchical relations between men and women and political authorities and subjects. In engagement with Milton (chap. 3), I showed that a critique of striving for superiority can be radical even if one affirms a hierarchical ordering of the world with natural superiors and inferiors.

3. Quoted in Hellerman, *Reconstructing Honor in Ancient Philippi*, 35. Cicero would not have wanted the pursuit of honor to be detached from other virtues or from seeking the common good; it was not purely honor for the sake of honor—but it is still noteworthy the significance he ascribes to honor. For a recent treatment in more depth than I can give here, see Schofield, *Cicero*.

4. For the scandal of social distinctions during the Lord's Supper as the problem being addressed in 1 Cor. 12:22–26, see Fee, *First Epistle to the Corinthians*, 678.

5. See the famous speech of Menenius Agrippa in Livy, *Early History of Rome*, 2.32.7–33.1. For discussion, see Schottroff, *1 Corinthians*, 253.

6. Luther, "Chapter Twelve," 455.

7. Luther, "Chapter Twelve," 455 (emphasis added). In a personal comment, Mark Seifrid reminded me that this is early Luther lecturing in 1515–16, before his Reformation discovery, who at the time still advocated a theology of humility, self-nullification, and divine elevation.

8. A variation of thinking less of oneself than of the other is John Albert Bengel's suggestion that "we rather consider the good qualities of others and our own faults" in *Gnomon of the New Testament*, 165. The comparative judgment would tend to be distorted.

9. I take the "honor" here to be not primarily about the objective worth of a person's achievement and possessions but about their worth *as a person*.

10. See my comments below on these passages.

11. Luther, "Chapter Twelve," 455.

12. "Mutual" or "one another" is one of the most widely used terms in Paul's ecclesiology and ethical instruction. See Lohfink, *Wie hat Jesus Gemeinde gewollt?*, 116ff.

13. What it means in practice to relate to others as if they were more important than oneself differs from culture to culture and may be a bit complicated in multicultural ecclesial communities. It may be that some forms of honoring may not be defensible on moral grounds. This complicates living by the principle but does not invalidate it.

14. Barth, *Epistle to the Philippians*, 56.

15. Kathryn Tanner made this point in a response to a previous version of this text.

182

16. Barth argues that the "edge would be taken off the argument if it were really to be translated: *also* that of others" (Barth, *Epistle to the Philippians*, 57–58). I am not persuaded. The contrast Paul draws is between holding someone (the other) "higher" and oneself "lower," not between holding someone for "something" and oneself for "nothing." The self does not need to disappear completely in regarding others as superior. As Barth himself notes, no surrender of the self is involved in seeking the interests of others, in the humility of which Paul writes, "the head should be held high" (57). The parallel with 2:21 is instructive. Writing about those around him who may be genuinely concerned for the Philippians, he notes that, except for Timothy, "all of them are seeking their own interests, not those of Jesus Christ." Seeking the interests of Jesus Christ *is* seeking the interests of the Philippians—and of all who belong to Christ, which includes the seeker of the interests of Christ as well.

17. Barth, *Epistle to the Philippians*, 56.

18. Personal correspondence, January 15 and 24, 2024.

19. Hellerman, *Reconstructing Honor in Ancient Philippi*, 130.

20. Stephen Fowl rightly notes that "grasping" is not about Christ's becoming or not becoming equal to God but about a certain "disposition or attitude toward" the divine status that is assumed he possesses. Fowl, "Christology and Ethics," 142.

21. A long tradition sees in this text some form of the Son's emptying himself of divinity in becoming human. I think this is an exegetical mistake. Whatever the implications of the entire hymn are for how we think about the divinity of Jesus Christ, Paul is most likely claiming not that Christ emptied himself of something but simply that Christ emptied *himself*. See Fee, *First Epistle to the Corinthians*, 210.

22. On the shame of crucifixion, see Hengel, *Crucifixion in the Ancient World*.

23. Hellerman, *Reconstructing Honor in Ancient Philippi*, 154–55.

24. Nietzsche, *Human, All Too Human I*, in *Complete Works*, vol. 3, §87. I owe this reference to Ryan McAnnally-Linz.

25. For Karl Barth, in his commentary on Philippians and elsewhere, exaltation does not come "after" humiliation. His argument is that "there is no mention of any resumption of the 'form of God'" (Barth, *Epistle to the Philippians*, 66). But what can giving the exalted Christ "the name that is above every name" mean but that the one who was and remained equal to God throughout the process, who had the form—the appearance—of God, is now recognized also in his apparently shameful deed as such? As I see it, exaltation means that also this disfigured "human form" is the form of God, not that he does not appear in any other form except that of the crucified slave. Not "He is in humility the highest" (62), as Barth interprets the text, but "Also in humility, he is the highest."

26. For a similar theme in John's Gospel, where crucifixion is rendered as glorification, though without denying the glory of the resurrection, see Volf and McAnnally-Linz, *Home of God*, 150, 184. We argue that the incarnation of the Son, whose earthly sojourn ended on the cross and is rendered as glorification, was foreshadowed in Exodus when "the glory of the LORD filled the tabernacle" (40:34). The point in John is that even in his greatest humiliation, the Son was glorified.

27. Luther, "Magnificat," 299–300.

28. The distinction between ascribed and achieved was first proposed in Linton, *Study of Man*, 115–31.

29. Hellerman, *Reconstructing Honor in Ancient Philippi*, 124–25.

30. Commenting on my text Matthew Croasmun notes the connection between elevation in status and belonging: "To indulge in psychologizing, I think Paul is seeking here belonging through striving for superiority. Especially as a bi-cultural

child, Paul is out of place both in Tarsus and in Jerusalem and sees the same status games regulating belonging—and keeping him outside. He goes all in on Pharisaism as a way of trying to establish his belonging in the people of his ancestors. And when that ends up putting him in opposition to God, he sees that the whole system of striving is for naught. Hence the revolution that begins on the road to Damascus. From there on out, his passion is to establish a new community (the church) in which belonging works entirely differently. And threats to that draw his sharpest critiques." Croasmun, personal communication with author, January 31, 2024.

31. Luther, *Freedom of the Christian*, 343–77.

32. In response to an earlier version of this chapter, Mark Seifrid wrote, "Do I lower myself now only in order to receive glory in the end? Is it not that our imitation (Phil. 3:17) of Christ takes place within the pattern of conformation to him in which we have been placed (3:20, and again, the reading of 2:5)?" Seifrid, personal communication with author, January 24, 2024.

33. A similar inclusive use of the race metaphor and the victor's prize is found in 2 Timothy 4:7–8: "I have finished the race. . . . From now on there is reserved for me the crown of righteousness, which the Lord, the righteous judge, will give me on that day, and not only to me but also to all who have longed for his appearing." I owe this reference to Tiago de Melo Novais.

34. Nietzsche, *Twilight of the Idols*, 121–22, in *Complete Works*, vol. 9.

35. This is one of the critical texts in the debate between the more traditional reading of Paul and the so-called New Perspectives on Paul (represented most ably by Richard Hays and N. T. Wright). I find a modified traditional reading—in fact, a modified version of Luther's interpretation of Paul—more compelling. In the comments on Romans that follow, I rely on Gathercole, *Where Is Boasting?*

36. See Luther, "Two Kinds of Righteousness," 297.

37. Gathercole, *Where Is Boasting?*, chap. 7.

38. Gathercole, *Where Is Boasting?*, chap. 7.

39. Teresa Morgan, personal communication, January 16, 2024.

40. See Luther, "Preface to the Epistle of St. Paul to the Romans," 370–71.

41. Gathercole, *Where Is Boasting?*, chap. 7.

42. On trust rather than faith, see Morgan, *New Testament and the Theology of Trust*.

## Chapter 5  "What Do You Have That You Did Not Receive?" (Paul)

1. In one of Luther's most formative early texts, "The Heidelberg Disputation," he distinguishes between "theology of the cross" and "theology of glory" (53). I apply the term to the theology of Paul's critics in Corinth, following Fee, *First Epistle to the Corinthians*, 192.

2. I follow here the translation in Fee, *First Epistle to the Corinthians*, 186.

3. Kierkegaard, *Philosophical Fragments*, 64–65.

4. This conjecture rests on the assumption that the Apollos party is the group of Corinthians who are not wise by human standards, nor powerful or noble (1 Cor. 1:27), and that Paul addresses them in 4:8.

5. See Nietzsche, *On the Genealogy of Morality* 1.10.

6. For the term "structure of bragging" that is "the wisdom of the world," see Schottroff, *1 Corinthians*, 52.

7. Nietzsche, *On the Genealogy of Morality* 1.15.

8. For taking "righteousness and sanctification and redemption" as explicating "wisdom," see Fee, *First Epistle to the Corinthians*, 89.

9. Along with many commentators (for instance, Fee, *First Epistle to the Corinthians*, 179; and Schottroff, *1 Corinthians*, 73), I opt for the alternative translation offered by the NRSVue.

10. Describing the Christian life through his own experience, Paul writes in 2 Corinthians 6:8–10, "We are treated as impostors and yet are true, as unknown and yet are well known, as dying and look—we are alive, as punished and yet not killed, as sorrowful yet always rejoicing, as poor yet making many rich, as having nothing and yet possessing everything."

11. As many other translations, the NRSVue has "What then is Apollos? What is Paul?" I have followed textual variants that instead of *ti* (what) have *tis* (who). In his commentary, Fee, a textual critic, uses mainly contextual reasons—the fact that, in his opinion, the context emphasizes functions rather than personalities of the two—to prefer neuter form to masculine, which is well attested in manuscripts (see Fee, *First Epistle to the Corinthians*, 137n344). My sense is that context emphasizes personalities, as it is about striving for superiority, and in giving answer to the questions, Paul states that neither he nor Apollos is anything. The issue is their status more than their functions.

12. Dale Martin notes that some forms of slavery and servanthood bestowed tremendous honor. Martin, *Slavery as Salvation*, chap. 1.

13. "We be his [Christ's] crown," Julian of Norwich claims in *Revelations of Divine Love*, chap. 12. I owe the reference to Ryan McAnnally-Linz.

14. The last phrase is from Drew Collins.

15. Bohnoeffer, "Who Am I?," 459–60. I owe the reference to Mark Seifrid.

16. Scholars debate about how many letters Paul wrote to the Corinthian church and whether 2 Corinthians, as we have it, is a single letter or a combination of two or more letters.

17. Some translations and commentaries take Paul's talk about not boasting "beyond [proper] limits" (2 Cor. 10:13) to implicitly allow boasting within limits. Mark Seifrid rejects, rightly in my opinion, the position: "Paul is not criticizing excessive boasting, he is insisting on eccentric boasting," which is "boasting in the Lord." Seifrid, *Second Letter to the Corinthians*, 392.

18. Bultmann, "καυχάομαι," 651. On Paul's boasting of his own work in general, Bultmann writes, "The basic rejection of self-glorying is not contradicted by passages in which Paul boasts of his work" (650). Paul is also not engaging in comparison in a very few other instances where he uses "boasting" positively (e.g., 1 Cor. 9:15; 15:31; 2 Cor. 11:10; Rom. 5:1–5; Phil. 2:16), all of which are, arguably, compatible with his stricture that the one who boasts must boast in the Lord rather than in themselves. On Paul's boasting of his own work in general, Rudolph Bultmann writes, "The basic rejection of self-glorying is not contradicted by passages in which Paul boasts of his work." Bultmann, "καυχάομαι," 650.

19. See Wright, "Lecture Nine." In Wright's view, the upside-down boast is fine.

20. There is one fascinating boast that Paul makes and on which he twice insists, and both times adamantly. He boasts that he proclaims the gospel to the Corinthians freely, writing, "As the truth of Christ is in me, this boast of mine will not be silenced in the regions of Achaia," which is where Corinth is located (2 Cor. 11:10). He makes a similar claim in 1 Corinthians 9:15: "No one will deprive me of my ground for boasting!" It is not that he is, in principle, opposed to receiving support from churches. He explicitly states that he has the right to do so (1 Cor. 9:3–14). He is, in fact, receiving support from other churches, and he is receiving it *while* he is in

Corinth (2 Cor. 11:9), but he refuses to receive it from the Corinthians themselves. He writes, "I will not be a burden because I do not want what is yours but you, for children ought not to save up for their parents but parents for their children. I will most gladly spend and be spent for you. If I love you more, am I to be loved less?" (12:14–15). With this last comment, he might have put his finger on the central problem. Commenting on the issue, Victor Furnish writes:

> Within Roman society specifically—and the Corinth Paul knew was a Roman colony—the wealthy expressed and enhanced their power by becoming patrons of the needy. The extent of one's philanthropies and the number of one's clients were important measures of a person's social standing and influence. . . . Therefore, to accept a gift was to become a client of and dependent upon the more privileged person, even though the patron, too, assumed the obligation of further benefaction. (Furnish, *II Corinthians*, 507)

One of the reasons why the Corinthians might have been upset that Paul was rejecting their financial support, Furnish suggests, was that in relationship to Paul they may have been after "power and prestige" (507). If so, by insisting on supporting himself and receiving help from elsewhere, he was resisting the idea that his preaching and teaching of the gospel of the crucified Christ be the means by which his hearers pursued their striving for superiority. Was he saying, "I am going to boast in my independence so as to prevent you from making my dependence on you an occasion for you to boast in your own superiority"?

21. See Wright, "Lecture Nine."

22. As I noted earlier, the idea is not that one is nothing, pure and simple, but that one is nothing *in oneself*. Paul writes, "I am not at all inferior to these super-apostles, even though I am nothing" (2 Cor. 12:11; see also 6:10).

23. For a theological analysis of the social critique of Rome in Revelation, see Volf and McAnnally-Linz, *Home of God*, 194–204.

24. Nietzsche, *Thus Spoke Zarathustra*, in *Portable Nietzsche*, 308; Scheler, *Ressentiment*, 57–61; Taylor, *Sources of the Self*, 63–73.

25. Plato, *Crito* 49d, in *Plato: Complete Works*, 44.

## Chapter 6 From Jesus to Genesis

1. Theissen, *Religion of the Earliest Churches*, 90.

2. See Levenson, *Death and Resurrection of the Beloved Son*.

3. Matthew Croasmun suggested this idea to me in personal correspondence from August 5, 2024. If this were the case, Mark would be promoting a similar notion of glory that we find in John's Gospel: Jesus being lifted up is his being glorified. See Volf and McAnnally-Linz, *Home of God*, 95–96.

4. See Volf, *Exclusion and Embrace*, 358–60.

5. Theissen argues that the idea of mutuality in renunciation of status was introduced in epistolary literature. Theissen, *Religion in Earliest Churches*, chap. 4. I would argue that the mutuality becomes explicit in epistolary literature, whereas in the Gospels it is implicit.

6. See Volf and McAnnally-Linz, *Home of God*, 213–14.

7. John's Gospel underscores that, by washing the feet of his disciples, Jesus is not seeking to gain in status by serving. The work of washing feet was at the time deemed so humiliating that Jewish slave owners were forbidden from compelling their slaves to do it. John introduces Jesus's foot washing, a job of the lowest of the low, by prefacing it with affirmation of his highest possible status: "Jesus, knowing that the Father had

given all things into his hands and that he had come from God and was going to God" (John 13:3). Exaltation is not reward for humble service; humble service is an expression of the exalted status. Jesus does not get exalted because he serves. He decides to serve as the one who is exalted, and in the act of service he is as exalted as he is on his throne. On humiliation and glorification in John, see Volf and McAnnally-Linz, *Home of God*, 92–96, 107–108. This parallels Phil. 2:6–11 (see chap. 4).

8. For a critique of striving for superiority in the Hebrew Bible, see Held, *Judaism Is about Love*, 30–32. For a treatment of the topic in popular Orthodox Jewish literature, see Kestenbaum, *Run after the Right Kavod*, 19–29. In his own terminology, Kestenbaum distinguishes between striving for excellence and striving for superiority, as I have done (see chap. 1).

9. Levenson, *Love of God*, 43.

10. In Genesis, God acts in seemingly arbitrary ways. God's treatment of Cain and Abel—a striving-for-superiority story, as I have mentioned earlier—is one such example. "In the course of time Cain brought to the LORD an offering of the fruit of the ground, and Abel for his part brought of the firstlings of his flock, their fat portions. And the LORD had regard for Abel and his offering, but for Cain and his offering he had no regard" (4:3–5). No reason is given for God's preference.

11. Levenson, *Inheriting Abraham*, 18–35.

12. Levenson, *Love of God*, 41. In Deuteronomy, the love of God for Israel has a shadow side. It is evident in the verses preceding the declaration of unmerited love and commitment to Israel. God will "clear away many nations" from the land Israel is to occupy. Israel should "utterly destroy them," for otherwise Israel will succumb to the temptation "to serve other gods," which would trigger God's anger against Israel and "he would destroy [them] quickly" (Deut. 7:1–4). For ways of dealing with the problem, see Levenson, *Love of God*, 38–41; and Held, *Judaism Is about Love*, 265–346.

13. Held, *Judaism Is about* Love, 311.

14. Levenson, *Love of God*, 45–46.

15. Sarna, *Genesis*, 13.

16. Mishnah Sanhedrin 4:5 (expanded translation), https://www.sefaria.org/Mishnah_Sanhedrin.4.5.

17. The story of creation of the first pair in Mishnah Sanhedrin 4:5 interpretation, like the call of Abraham and the election of Israel, are not explicitly about striving for superiority—they are about making *claims to superiority*. But if claims to superiority are disallowed, so must also be striving to be superior so as to be able to make claims to superiority.

18. Held, *Judaism Is about Love*, 31.

19. Held, *Heart of Torah*, 64–65.

20. Held, *Heart of Torah*, 66.

21. Levenson, "Genesis," 69.

22. Kaminsky, "Reclaiming a Theology of Election," 138.

23. Held, *Heart of Torah*, 85, quoting Kaminsky, "Reclaiming a Theology of Election," 139.

24. Held, *Heart of Torah*, 85.

25. Sarna, *Genesis*, 321; and Lerner, "Joseph the Unrighteous," 279.

26. Levenson, "Genesis," 87.

27. See Robinson, *Reading Genesis*, 15–17, 224–230.

28. Dostoevsky, *Crime and Punishment*, 158.

29. Wilson, *Does Altruism Exist?*

# Bibliography

Adler, Alfred. *The Best of Alfred Adler*. Grapevine India, 2023. Kindle.

Augustine. *The City of God against the Pagans*. Edited and translated by R. W. Dyson. Cambridge: Cambridge University Press, 1998.

Bardill, Jonathan. "A New Temple for Byzantium: Anicia Juliana, King Solomon, and the Gilded Ceiling of the Church of St. Polyeuktos in Constantinople." In *Social and Political Life in Late Antiquity*, edited by William Bowden, Adam Gutteridge, and Carlos Machado, 339–70. Leiden: Brill, 2006.

Barker, John W. *Justinian and the Later Roman Empire*. Madison: University of Wisconsin Press, 1966.

Barnaby, Andrew. "'The Form of a Servant': At(-)onement by Kenosis in *Paradise Lost*." *Milton Quarterly* 52, no. 1 (2018): 1–19.

Barth, Karl. *The Epistle to the Philippians*. Translated by James W. Leitch. Richmond, VA: John Knox Press, 1962.

Bell, Peter N., trans. *Three Political Voices from the Age of Justinian*. Liverpool: Liverpool University Press, 2009.

Bengel, John Albert. *Gnomon of the New Testament*. Vol. 3, *Romans and 1 and 2 Corinthians*. Translated by James Bryce. Edinburgh: T&T Clark, 1877.

Bertram, Christopher. "Jean-Jacques Rousseau." *Stanford Encyclopedia of Philosophy*. Stanford University. First published September 27, 2010. Revised April 21, 2023. https://plato.stanford.edu/entries/rousseau.

Blake, William. *The Marriage of Heaven and Hell*. Boston: John W. Luce and Company, 1906.

Bloom, Harold. *The Anxiety of Influence: A Theory of Poetry*. Oxford: Oxford University Press, 1973.

Bonhoeffer, Dietrich. "Who Am I?" In *Dietrich Bonhoeffer Works*, vol. 8, *Letters and Papers from Prison*, edited by John W. de Gruchy, 459–60. Minneapolis: Fortress, 2010.

Bultmann, Rudolph. "καυχάομαι." In *Theological Dictionary of the New Testament*, vol. 3, edited by Gerhard Kittle and Gerhard Friedrich, 645–54. Grand Rapids: Eerdmans, 1964–76.

Chapais, Bernard. "Competence and the Evolutionary Origins of Status and Power in Humans." *Human Nature* 26 (2015): 161–83.

Charvet, John. *The Social Problem in the Philosophy of Jean-Jacques Rousseau*. Cambridge: Cambridge University Press, 1974.

Cheng, Joey T., Jessical L. Tracy, and Joseph Henrich, "Pride, Personality, and the Evolutionary Foundations of Human Social Status." *Evolution and Human Behavior* 31, no. 5 (2010): 334–47.

Cohen, Paula Maranz. "Injured Merit: How a Righteous Sense of Grievance Can Lead to a Better World." *American Scholar*, January 28, 2021. https://theamericanscholar.org/injured-merit.

Cortina, Adela. *Aporophobia: Why We Reject the Poor Instead of Helping Them*. Princeton: Princeton University Press, 2022.

De Benoist, Alain. *On Being a Pagan*. Translated by John Graham. North Augusta, SC: Arcana Europa Media, 2018.

Dostoevsky, Fyodor. *Crime and Punishment*. Translated by Richard Pevear and Larissa Volokhonsky. New York: Vintage, 2021.

Ehrenberg, Alain. *The Weariness of the Self: Diagnosing the History of Depression in the Contemporary Age*. Montreal: McGill-Queen's University Press, 2009.

Falcone, Filippo. *Milton's Inward Liberty: A Reading of Christian Liberty from the Prose to Paradise Lost*. Eugene, OR: James Clark, 2014.

Fee, Gordon. *The First Epistle to the Corinthians*. Grand Rapids: Eerdmans, 2014.

Fowl, Stephen E. "Christology and Ethics in Philippians 2:5–11." In *Where Christology Began: Essays on Philippians 2*, edited by Ralph P. Martin and Brian J. Dodd, 140–53. Louisville: Westminster John Knox, 1998.

Frías, Francisco Javier López. "Games as Windows and Remedies to Modern Society: A Qualified Defense of Agonistic Encounters." Yale Center for Faith & Culture, Consultation on "Striving for Superiority," New Haven, CT, December 8–9, 2023.

Furnish, Victor Paul. *II Corinthians: Translated with Introduction, Notes and Commentary*. Anchor Bible 32A. Garden City, NY: Doubleday, 1984.

Galbraith, John Kenneth. *The Affluent Society*. Boston: Houghton Mifflin, 1959.

Gathercole, Simon J. *Where Is Boasting? Early Jewish Soteriology and Paul's Response in Romans 1–5*. Grand Rapids: Eerdmans, 2002. Kindle.

Gilbert, Sandra M. "Patriarchal Poetry and Women Readers: Reflections on Milton's Bogey." *Publications of the Modern Language Association (PMLA)* 93, no. 3 (May 1978): 368–82. https://www.jstor.org/stable/461860.

"The Hagia Sophia Case." *Harvard Law Review* 134, no. 3 (January 2021): 1278–85. https://harvardlawreview.org/print/vol-134/the-hagia-sophia-case.

Han, Byung-Chul. *The Burnout Society*. Translated by Erik Butler. Stanford, CA: Stanford University Press, 2015.

Harrison, R. M. "The Church of St. Polyeuktos in Istanbul and the Temple of Solomon." *Harvard Ukrainian Studies* 7 (January 1983): 276–79.

Hawkins, Justin. "Pusillanimity, Superiority, Magnanimity, Haecceity: A Reply to Miroslav Volf." Yale Center for Faith & Culture, Consultation on "Striving for Superiority," September 9–10, 2022.

Held, Shai. *The Heart of Torah*. Vol. 1, *Essays on the Weekly Torah Portion: Genesis and Exodus*. Philadelphia: Jewish Publication Society, 2017.

———. *Judaism Is about Love: Recovering the Heart of Jewish Life*. New York: Farrar, Straus and Giroux, 2024.

Hellerman, Joseph H. *Reconstructing Honor in Ancient Philippi: Carmen Christi as Cursus Pudorum*. Cambridge: Cambridge University Press, 2005.

Hengel, Martin. *Crucifixion in the Ancient World and the Folly of the Message of the Cross*. Translated by John Bowden. Philadelphia: Fortress, 1977.

Hobbes, Thomas. *The Elements of Law, Natural and Politic*. Edited by Ferdinand Tönnies. London: Frank Cass, 1969.

Homer. *The Odyssey of Homer*. Translated by Richmond Lattimore. New York: HarperCollins, 2007.

Hunter, William B. "Milton on the Exaltation of the Son: The War in Heaven in *Paradise Lost*." *English Literary History* 36, no. 1 (March 1969): 215–31.

Janezic, Katharina A., and Aina Gallego. "Eliciting Preferences for Truth-Telling in a Survey of Politicians." *Proceedings of the National Academy of Sciences of the United States of America* 117, no. 36 (August 2020): 22002–22008. https://doi.org/10.1073/pnas.2008144117.

Johnston, James E. "Milton on the Doctrine of the Atonement." *Renascence* 38, no. 1 (Autumn 1985): 40–53.

Julian of Norwich. *Revelations of Divine Love*. Translated by Barry Windeatt. Oxford: Oxford University Press, 2015.

Kaminsky, Joel S. "Reclaiming a Theology of Election: Favoritism and the Joseph Story." *Perspectives in Religious Studies* 31, no. 2 (Summer 2004): 135–52.

Kant, Immanuel. *Religion within the Boundaries of Mere Reason*. Edited by Allen Wood and George di Giovanni. Cambridge: Cambridge University Press, 1998.

Kavanagh, Jennifer, and Michael D. Rich. *Truth Decay: An Initial Exploration of the Diminishing Role of Facts and Analysis in American Public Life*. Santa Monica, CA: RAND, 2018.

Kestenbaum, Moshe Don. *Run after the Right Kavod: Changing the World—and Yourself!—through Proper Use of Respect, Self-Esteem, and Honor*. Lakewood, NJ: Israel Bookshop, 2011.

Kiechel, Walter. "The Case against Competing." *Harvard Business Review*, April 30, 2015. https://hbr.org/2015/04/the-case-against-competing.

Kierkegaard, Søren. *Christian Discourses*. Edited and translated by Howard V. Hong and Edna H. Hong. Princeton: Princeton University Press, 1997.

———. *Without Authority*. Vol. 18 of *Kierkegaard's Writings*. Translated by Howard V. Hong and Edna H. Hong. Princeton: Princeton University Press, 1997.

———. *Philosophical Fragments*. Translated by David F. Swenson and Howard V. Hong. Princeton: Princeton University Press, 1962.

———. *Practice in Christianity*. Edited and translated by Howard V. Hong and Edna H. Hong. Princeton: Princeton University Press, 1991.

———. *The Sickness unto Death: A Christian Psychological Exposition for Upbuilding and Awakening*. Edited and translated by Howard V. Hong and Edna H. Hong. Princeton: Princeton University Press, 1980.

———. *Upbuilding Discourses in Various Spirits*. Edited and translated by Howard V. Hong and Edna H. Hong. Princeton: Princeton University Press, 1993.

———. *Works of Love*. Translated by Howard V. Hong and Edna H. Hong. Princeton: Princeton University Press, 1995.

Kilgour, Maggie. "'Thy Perfect Image Viewing': Poetic Creation and Ovid's Narcissus in *Paradise Lost*." *Studies in Philology* 102, no. 3 (Summer 2005): 307–39.

Labriola, Albert C. "'Thy Humiliation Shall Exalt': The Christology of *Paradise Lost*." *Milton Studies* 15 (1981): 29–42.

Levenson, Jon D. *The Death and Resurrection of the Beloved Son: Transformation of Child Sacrifice in Judaism and Christianity*. New Haven: Yale University Press, 1995.

———. "Genesis." In *The Jewish Study Bible*, 2nd ed., edited by Adele Berlin and Marc Zvi Brettler, 10–94. New York: Oxford University Press, 2014.

———. *Inheriting Abraham: The Legacy of the Patriarch in Judaism, Christianity, and Islam*. Princeton: Prenceton University Press, 2012.

———. *The Love of God: Divine Gift, Human Gratitude, and Mutual Faithfulness in Judaism*. Princeton: Princeton University Press, 2016.

Lerner, Berel Dov. "Joseph the Unrighteous." *Judaism* 38 (1989): 278–81.

Lewis, C. S. *A Preface to Paradise Lost: Being the Ballard Matthews Lectures Delivered at University College, North Wales, 1941*. London: Oxford University Press, 1954.

Linton, Ralph. *The Study of Man*. New York: Appleton-Century-Crofts, 1936.

Lippitt, John, and C. Stephen Evans. "Søren Kierkegaard." *Stanford Encyclopedia of Philosophy*. Stanford University. First published December 3, 1996. Last modified November 10, 2017. https://plato.stanford.edu/archives/spr2023/entries/kierkegaard.

Livy. *The Early History of Rome, Books I–V*. Translated by Aubrey de Sélincourt. New York: Penguin Classics, 2002.

Lohfink, Gerhard. *Wie hat Jesus Gemeinde gewollt? Zur gesellschaftlichen Dimension des christlichen Glaubens*. Freiburg: Herder, 1982.

Löwith, Karl. *Von Hegel zu Nietzsche: Der revolutionäre Bruch im Denken des 19. Jahrhunderds*. Hamburg: Felix Meiner Verlag, 1969.

Luthar, Suniya S., and Nina L. Kumar. "Youth in High-Achieving Schools: Challenges to Mental Health and Directions for Evidence-Based Interventions." In *Handbook of School-Based Mental Health Promotion: An Evidence-Informed Framework for Implementation*, edited by Alan W. Leschied, Donald H. Saklofske, and Gordon L. Flett, 441–58. New York: Springer Science, 2018.

Luther, Martin. *The Freedom of the Christian*. In *Luther's Works*, vol. 31, *Career of the Reformer I*, edited by Harold J. Grimm and Helmut T. Lehmann, translated by W. A. Lambert, 327–78. Philadelphia: Muhlenberg, 1957.

———. "The Heidelberg Disputation, 1518." In *Luther's Works*, vol. 31, *Career of the Reformer I*, edited and translated by Harold J. Grimm, 35–70. Philadelphia: Fortress, 1957.

———. *Lectures on Romans*. In *Luther's Works*, vol. 25, edited by Hilton C. Oswald, 433–67. St. Louis: Concordia, 1972.

———. "The Magnificat." In *Luther's Works*, vol. 21, *Sermon on the Mount and the Magnificat*, edited by Jaroslav Jan Pelikan and translated by A. T. Steinhaeuser, 295–355. St. Louis: Concordia, 1956.

———. "Preface to the Epistle of St. Paul to the Romans." In *Luther's Works*, vol. 34, *Word and Sacrament I*, edited by E. Theodore Bachmann and Helmut T. Lehmann, translated by Charles M. Jacobs, 365–80. Philadelphia: Muhlenberg, 1960.

———. "Two Kinds of Righteousness, 1519." In *Luther's Works*, vol. 31, *Career of the Reformer I*, edited by Harold J. Grimm and translated by Lowell J. Satre, 293–306. Philadelphia: Fortress, 1957.

Martin, Dale. *Slavery as Salvation: The Metaphor of Slavery in Pauline Christianity*. New Haven: Yale University Press, 1990.

McClanan, Anne. *Representations of Early Byzantine Empresses: Image and Empire*. New York: Palgrave MacMillan, 2002.

Meier, Heinrich. "Rousseaus Diskurs über den Ursprung und die Grundlagen der Ungleichheit unter den Menschen: Ein einführender Essay über die Rhetorik und die Intention des Werkes." In *Diskurs über die Ungleichheit*, by Jean-Jacques Rousseau, edited by Heinrich Maier, xxi–lxvii. Paderborn: UTB, Stuttgart, 2001.

Milton, John. *Complete Poems and Major Prose*. Edited by Merritt Y. Hughes. Indianapolis: Hackett, 2003.

———. *Paradise Lost*. Edited by William Kerrigan, John Rumrich, and Stephen M. Fallon. New York: Modern Library, 2008.

———. "The Tenure of Kings and Magistrates." In *John Milton: Complete Poems and Major Prose*, edited by Merritt Y. Hughes (Indianapolis: Hackett, 2003).

Morgan, Teresa. *The New Testament and the Theology of Trust: "This Rich Trust."* Oxford: Oxford University Press, 2022.

Morrison, Toni. *The Bluest Eye*. New York: Vintage, 2007.

Neuhouser, Frederick. *Rousseau's Theodicy of Self-Love: Evil, Rationality, and the Drive for Recognition*. Oxford: Oxford University Press, 2009.

Nietzsche, Friedrich. *The Complete Works of Friedrich Nietzsche*. Edited by Alan D. Schrift, Duncan Large, and Adrian Del Caro. Stanford, CA: Stanford University Press, 2021.

———. *Nietzsche: On the Genealogy of Morality and Other Writings*. Edited by Keith Ansell-Pearson. Translated by Carol Diethe. Cambridge: Cambridge University Press, 2017.

———. *The Portable Nietzsche*. Translated by Walter Kaufmann. New York: Penguin, 1976.

———. *The Will to Power*. Translated by Walter Kaufmann and R. J. Hollingdale. New York: Vintage, 1968.

Ousterhout, Robert G. *Eastern Medieval Architecture: The Building Traditions of Byzantium and Neighboring Lands*. Onassis Series in Hellenic Culture. New York: Oxford University Press, 2019.

Ovid. *Metamorphoses*. Translated by A. D. Melville. Oxford: Oxford University Press, 2009.

*Oxford English Dictionary*. 2nd ed. Oxford: Oxford University Press, 2004.

Pattison, Mark. "Milton." In *John Milton: Complete Poetical Works*. Hastings, East Sussex: Delphi Classics, 2015. Kindle.

Phillips, Edward. "The Life of Milton." In *Complete Poems and Major Prose*, edited by Merritt Y. Hughes, 1025–37. Indianapolis: Hackett, 2003.

Plato. *Crito*. In *Plato: Complete Works*, edited by John Cooper and translated by G. M. A. Grube, 37–48. Indianapolis: Hackett, 1997.

———. *Republic*. In *Plato: Complete Works*, edited by John Cooper and translated by G. M. A. Grube and C. D. C. Reeve, 971–1223. Indianapolis: Hackett, 1997.

Plekon, Michael. "Moral Accounting: Kierkegaard's Social Theory and Criticism." *Kierkegaardiana* 12 (June 1982): 69–82, https://doi.org/10.7146/kga.v12i0.31357.

Plutarch. "Caesar." In *Roman Lives: A Selection of Eight Roman Lives*. Translated by Robin Waterfield. Oxford: Oxford University Press, 2009.

Roberts, Robert C. *Recovering Christian Character: The Psychological Wisdom of Søren Kierkegaard*. Grand Rapids: Eerdmans, 2022.

Robinson, Marilynne. *Reading Genesis*. New York: Farrar, Straus and Giroux, 2024.

Rogers, John. "The Infant Cry of God." English 220: Milton. Class lecture at Yale University, New Haven, CT, Fall 2007.

———. "*Paradise Lost*: Books V–VI." English 220: Milton. Class lecture at Yale University, New Haven, CT, Fall 2007.

Rosa, Hartmut. *Resonance: A Sociology of Our Relation to the World*. Translated by James C. Wagner. Cambridge: Polity Press, 2019.

———. *Social Acceleration: A New Theory of Modernity*. Translated by Jonathan Trejo-Mathys. New York: Columbia University Press, 2014.

Rousseau, Jean-Jacques. "Discourse on the Origin and the Foundation of Inequality among Men, or Second Discourse." In *Rousseau: The Discourses and Other Early Political Writings*, edited and translated by Victor Gourevitch, 111–231. Cambridge: Cambridge University Press, 2019.

Sandel, Michael J. *The Tyranny of Merit: What's Become of the Common Good*. New York: Farrar, Straus and Giroux, 2020.

Sarna, Nahum. *Genesis*. Philadelphia: Jewish Publication Society, 1989.

Scheler, Max. *Ressentiment*. Translated by Lewis B. Coser and William W. Holdheim. Milwaukee: Marquette University Press, 1988.

Schibille, Nadine. *Hagia Sophia and the Byzantine Aesthetic Experience*. New York: Ashgate, 2014.

Schofield, Malcolm. *Cicero: Political Philosophy*. Oxford: Oxford University Press, 2021.

Schottroff, Louise. *1 Corinthians*. Translated by Everett R. Kalin. Stuttgart: Kohlhammer Verlag, 2022.

Seifrid, Mark. *The Second Letter to the Corinthians*. Grand Rapids: Eerdmans, 2014.

Simmel, Georg. *Schriften zur Soziologie: Eine Auswahl*. Edited by Ottenhein Rammstedt and Heinz-Jürgen Dahme. Frankfurt am Main: Suhrkamp, 1983.

Smith, Adam. *The Theory of Moral Sentiments*. Uplifting Publications, 2009. Kindle.

Soulen, Kendall. Untitled paper. Yale Center for Faith & Culture, Consultation on "Striving for Superiority," September 9–10, 2022.

Stendahl, Krister. *Final Account: Paul's Letter to the Romans*. Minneapolis: Fortress, 1995.

Taylor, Charles. *Cosmic Connections: Poetry in the Age of Disenchantment*. Cambridge, MA: Belknap Press of Harvard University Press, 2024.

———. *Sources of the Self: The Making of the Modern Identity*. Cambridge, MA: Harvard University Press, 1989.

Theissen, Gerd. *The Religion of the Earliest Churches: Creating a Symbolic World*. Translated by John Bowden. Minneapolis: Fortress, 1999.

Urban, David V. "The Increasing Distance between *De Doctrina Christiana* and Milton's Poetry: An Answer to John K. Hale." *Connotations* 32 (April 2023): 1–10.

———. "Revisiting the History of the *De Doctrina Christiana* Authorship Debate and Its Ramifications for Milton Scholarship: A Response to Falcone and Kerr." *Connotations* 29, no. 2 (July 2020): 156–88.

US Surgeon General's Advisory. *Social Media and Youth Mental Health*. US Department of Health and Human Services, 2023. https://www.hhs.gov/sites/default/files/sg-youth-mental-health-social-media-advisory.pdf.

Virgil. *The Aeneid*. Translated by Robert Fitzgerald. New York: Vintage Books, 1990.

Volf, Miroslav. *Exclusion and Embrace: A Theological Exploration of Identity, Otherness, and Reconciliation*. Rev. ed. Nashville: Abingdom, 2019.

Volf, Miroslav, and Ryan McAnnally-Linz. *The Home of God: A Brief Story of Everything*. Grand Rapids: Brazos, 2022.

———. "Joyful Recognition: Debt, Duty, and Gratitude to God." In *A Theology of Gratitude: Christian and Muslim Perspectives*, edited by Mona Siddiqui and Nathanael Vette, 3–17. Cambridge: Cambridge University Press, 2023.

Wallace, David Foster. *This Is Water: Some Thoughts, Delivered on a Significant Occasion, about Living a Compassionate Life*. New York: Little, Brown, 2009.

Wilson, David Sloan. *Does Altruism Exist? Culture, Genes, and the Welfare of Others*. New Haven: Yale University Press, 2015.

Wright, N. T. "Lecture Nine: Paul's Upside-Down Boast: 2 Corinthians 11:16–12:13." Second Corinthians Webinar, Summer 2020.